To David
God bless you in your
ministry
Simon — your son in law — has
become a good friend

Matthew in *(signature)*
Your Pocket
A Pilgrimage With a Gospel

CW00551843

Bishop Martin Shaw

Saunton Press

Cover image © iStockphoto.com/MauMar70

The information in this book was believed to be correct at the time of writing. All content is for information purposes only and is not intended as legal advice. No liability is accepted by either the publisher or author for any errors or omissions (whether negligent or not) that it may contain. Professional advice should always be obtained before applying any information to particular circumstances.

Published 2017 by
Saunton Press
(an imprint of Law Brief Publishing)
30 The Parks
Minehead
Somerset
TA24 8BT

www.sauntonpress.com

Paperback: 978-1-911035-47-3

PREFACE

I'm inviting you to join me on a pilgrimage I'll be making with a friend of mine! This pilgrimage will be of the imagination, of the heart. I suppose in truth, it's a fictitious pilgrimage. My friend is none other than St Francis of Assisi. For me, the imagination's a vital and an exciting tool for reliving something of a saint's life. So I'll be, as it were, 'walking and talking' with you, through these pages, about the story of the pilgrimage which'll take who knows how long. At each stage, I'll have my own personal reflections and I'll be addressing you personally in the hope to make some connection with where you might be. The story of the pilgrimage, apart from walking, is mostly about ordinary experiences: eating, resting, talking, getting irritated, being bored, embarrassed, delighted: and any other mood you care to add.

I'll be picturing Francis, my friend and I hope yours also, carrying a copy of St Matthew's Gospel in his pocket, as I will myself. Maybe you'll do the same. Why Matthew's Gospel? Francis knew it well and he may have known much of it by heart. After all, he lived it! For me, I have had the privilege of singing many times the part of 'Christus' in J S Bach's 'St Matthew Passion', a work of art that reaches beyond art and even religious boundaries. Of the many experiences of Matthew's Gospel that has grasped me, there's the simple and disturbing portrayal of Jesus in Paulo

Pasolini's blunt and raw film: 'The Gospel according to St Matthew'. Pasolini filmed the Gospel 'head-on'. He deepened the poignant drama of the Gospel by using local, non-professional actors, as well as music from Bach's St Matthew Passion and the Missa Luba written in the Democratic Republic of Congo in the 1950s.

The word Gospel means simply 'God story'. The best of stories reveal underlying truths about human experience. To 'Gospel', using the word as a verb, is to tell the story of the experience of God here and now and what that will mean for the living of that Gospel, not just as an individual but as a community of those who feel drawn into being part of that story, that Gospel.

So, as you make your pilgrimage with me, I hope to show Francis using the Gospel as a means of experiencing Jesus' presence; his 'real presence' that goes beyond my ability to express in factual terms. The purpose of this little book is to provide some help for you to pray more deeply and, of course, love more deeply. There's been far too much ecclesiastical and theological encrustation around the gospels, endangering the experience of the radical Jesus of the Gospel in the present moment.

The author of 'St Matthew's Gospel' has a significant body of text in common with St Luke, which may suggest that there's another source which both authors used, so far unknown. He also used St Mark's Gospel, but a quarter of the text of St Matthew's Gospel is particular to it, giving specific attention to Jesus relationship with other Jews. The Hebrew Bible [which for ease and because of familiarity, I've called The Old Testament] is used with great authority and is treated reverently in Matthew. However, there are, for the author, some teachers among the Jews whom he describes as 'blind guides'. Jesus is presented as proclaiming a new approach to living in community and the moral implications of that living. The Sermon on the Mount is a collected guidance, almost a manual of hopeful encouragement for practicing the Christ-like life of gentleness, poverty of spirit, mercy and making peace. With confidence, Matthew portrays Jesus as the Messiah for the Jews, bringing into being what the Hebrew prophets had spoken and written. All this amounted to a Gospel that would be a significantly useful reference for the early Christian Church.

To walk with St Francis of Assisi, at least in my imagination, became the dynamic for the writing this little book, not least because in his short life, he walked up and down the length of Italy several times. In doing so, he was merely emulating Jesus' walking. Peregrinatio - Pilgrimage. Francis, or Francesco, 'the little Frenchman', was his nickname, given to him not only because of his father's trading in France, but because of Francis' own love for the songs and stories of the Troubadours, just across the Alps. Francis, whose given name was Giovanni di Pietro, was born in 1182 in the beautiful hill city Assisi, in central Italy's Umbria. He died in 1226 in a village called Santa Maria deli Angeli, in the long low valley below Assisi. Italy, at that time, was made up of a number of city states, some of which were at war with each other. Francis, having been something of a playboy, fought in a war with the neighbouring city of Perugia. He was captured and imprisoned for a year. When he returned to Assisi, it became clear that his priorities had to change. Today, it might be suggested that he suffered from post-traumatic stress, or some form of depression. His hopes for military glory led to nothing but dejection. He met a leper, who he realised was an example of being rejected like Christ himself. He took responsibility to care for the man and it's said that Francis even hugged and kissed him. Close by, there was a little church of San Damiano, which had fallen into disrepair. Francis distinctly heard a voice tell him to rebuild the church. Obeying the voice literally, he imagined the command to mean San Damiano. So he started to beg, borrow and steal materials for the rebuild. However, it became clear that 'rebuild my church' had a much wider implication.

The Franciscan Community eventually gathered pace by another little abandoned chapel, called the Porziuncula in the valley below. It's said that when Francis went into the chapel, the Gospel of Matthew was lying open on a reading desk at the passage from St Matthew chapter 16 verse 24: "Whoever wants to be my disciple must deny themselves and take up their cross and follow me." It's this story that has always intrigued me and, I suppose, brought about in my imagination the marriage of the Gospel of St Matthew and St Francis in the context of an imaginary walk, a pilgrimage.

Francis' prayer had an intensity to it, in that he wanted to identify with the wounds of Christ. Franciscan tradition shows that he received his answer. In Tuscany, on Monte la Verna, he received the five marks of the wounds of Christ, known as the stigmata. And this identifying intimately with the Passion of Christ was another incentive for me to make a pilgrimage with Francis through the Gospel and into the heart of the Passion. After all, Francis early rule for the brothers was quite simple: 'to follow in the footsteps of Jesus.'

Where this imagined pilgrimage starts and finishes, is a mystery, even to myself! You'll pick up a sense and perhaps even a direction of the pilgrimage through all the little encounters we will have together. The experience of walking, indeed any kind of travel, with people, old and new friends, and making the effort of the journey itself, with its geography, is at the heart of pilgrimage.

Throughout, I'll be using reference to the New Jerusalem Bible translation, because the Gospel of Matthew, in that version, is divided up into small convenient sections, to enable access, as well as careful and reflective reading and re-reading. Another advantage of this translation is that you can buy individual copies of the Gospel in a small light paperback version for your pocket. However, it may be that you'll have your own preferred version of the Gospel that has either helped you to experience the dynamic of your reading, or at least continues to provide you with the opportunity for an affective response. It doesn't matter too much if your version has the sections divided differently than the one I'm using. If you can, persist with the verse sections that I'll be giving as we go along.

Each of the sections in the twenty eight chapters of Matthew's Gospel, I'll use as a basis for meditation, beginning each time with a very short story of a particular experience on the imagined pilgrimage that I'll be having with Francis. Many of the little stories include conversations, mostly between Francis and myself, but also with others who we meet or join us on the way. The story of the pilgrimage is told in the present tense in order to create an atmosphere of immediacy. Your responses will, inevitably, be sometimes unique to you. I've tried to 'create space' for that to happen.

Following each little narrative, I give you the passage reference for each section of the Gospel. It's important, at this point, to take time to read the passage in your own copy at least twice before going any further. If you feel the slightest urge to stop at a word or a phrase, then do so. This is a book that I've designed to be used flexibly not to be rushed through. You'll be able to return to what I've written when it feels appropriate to do so. Meditation, like a pilgrimage, isn't a project to be completed, but an experience to be embraced and reflected upon. Being open to the movement of God is at the heart of meditation and not what someone, including myself, has written about it.

Then I'll give you a brief reflection on the passage that's not analytical but opens, I hope, possibilities of approach. For the most part, this part of each meditation is personal, as I want to avoid being caught in a theoretical approach to spirituality. Each meditation,,as a whole, will be much more about 'falling in love' with Jesus with all the confusions, uncertainties and even agonies, as well as delights or boredoms that go with falling in love. Let the gut respond as it will – or not, without judgement or examination.

At the heart of the meditation, I'll give you a sentence which has emerged from the particular Gospel section. For example: "Let My Love of You draw you into My Way and My Truth". The sentence will help you to move beyond the passage into a deeper inner place with the sentence, moving from the memory, the mind and 'into' the heart. Remember that it takes a while to settle into meditation. Furthermore, it's important to come out of the meditation with gentleness and care, in order that the meditation 'carry forward' into living.

The last section of the meditation will suggest ways in which a spiritual exercise might be useful either as part of one meditation period or at another time in the day.

You might ask at this stage in what way this book, this pilgrimage might help you with your praying and your loving. It's perhaps over-reaching myself to claim that what I write can help you live the Christ-like life. But I'll risk that it might be for some. Paradoxically, the life of praying is a deep and intimate love-affair with God, both delicate and strong. The hard graft of the work of praying is so because for most who take praying seriously it's a work of living with dryness, coping with the depth of human emotion and feeling, as well as intrusive distractions, some pleasant, some not.

In praying, there's an asking, indeed perhaps even a nagging of God, as this little book will suggest. But that praying is not about God changing the circumstances of mine or anyone else's life, but allowing a deep inner life to be an environment of healing, where the Light of Christ can work. That will enable you to respond to the conscious and unconscious depths within you, that in the mystery of the humility of Christ and the constant 'breathing' of the Spirit, Love can be realised in the practice of waiting, patience and gentle strength. It's from the work of meditation that you are enabled in the practice of loving, in order that you may perhaps, live at least some of your life as if you're dependent on God. So, join me in the pilgrimage and don't forget to put Matthew in your pocket.

This little book may be used in various circumstances, maybe even on a specific pilgrimage; for example, you may be planning to walk to Santiago de Compostela, or some other pilgrimage route. This little book, with 'Matthew in Your Pocket', may help you to deepen the experience. Or you may want to use some of it on a retreat, or on several retreats or quiet days. For the most part, I expect that you may want to use it daily in your own practice of praying. Opening the book at the beginning of any meditation will work as well, but I hope you make the journey with the Gospel as a whole, for you will make surprising new friends and, perhaps, be lifted a little higher in your awareness of Christ's presence as you journey towards Christ's passion and his raising, the resurrection.

Martin Shaw
March 2017

ACKNOWLEDGEMENTS

This little book owes much to the encouragement and feedback from members of the Third Order of the Society of St Francis in Devon. So in thanking them, I also must thank my dear wife Elspeth, who has gently persuaded me to return to the task when I had periods of flagging. Tim Kevan, who has been instrumental to the publishing of 'Matthew in Your Pocket', I thank for his patience, encouragement and suggestions.

The style of the book has arisen from what I've experienced and learnt from many sources, particularly the Fellowship of Meditation. For many years, I've had the privilege of leading pilgrimages to Assisi, where the creative atmosphere for the imaginary stories I've told about Francis in the book were germinated. The gift of a walking pilgrimage and of distance come from my pilgrimages to Santiago de Compostela from Leon and Oporto, respectively.

The inspiration for what lies behind the spirituality of this little book comes from the writing of Richard Holloway, whose clarity, learning, compassion as well as observation have accompanied me and excited me throughout my adult life. Dietrich Bonhoeffer's depth and yet simplicity in writing about the simple and costly obedience that is essential for following Christ, has been a constant challenge in returning to the core of Matthew's Gospel. Søren Kierkegaard and Simone

Weil, have helped me to understand that the dangers of organisations, particularly religious ones, to allow power and prominence to distort the simplicity of the Gospel must be challenged. However, Rowan Williams, in his poetry as well as his preaching, lecturing and other writing, has also reminded me of the beauty of the Church, as a geographically and non-geographically placed source of friendship and acceptance through the sacraments of the Eucharist and, for me, the healing that confession and absolution brings, which, in embryonic form are there in the Gospel of Matthew.

So, if you have your kit ready, and checked that you've the Gospel of Matthew in your pocket, we'll get going.

Contents

CHAPTER ONE – MATTHEW 1

1.

THE PILGRIMAGE

Francis and I agree to meet down by a five-way junction on our long path, where we'll start our pilgrimage together. Why the pilgrimage? I have to confess, that I don't really know. There is, of course, the opportunity of being with Francis himself. A week ago, he reminded me that I must bring with me a copy of St Matthew's Gospel. "Just stick it your pocket. You'll need it along the way," says Francis with a wink. "What else will I need?" "Well, not much, if the Gospel is to be followed. Use your common sense. Apart from anything else, what you don't have with you, you can scrounge."

So, I think to myself, "What if don't get back; illness, accident or maybe I'll just stay wherever it is that we land up". So, I write on the inside of my Matthew, the names of as many of my family and friends as I could remember. Francis asks me about the marks on my staff. "That's where we'll start".

Read the section: Matthew 1:1-17

THE REFLECTION

While learning to know Christ in prayer with Matthew's Gospel, the names of the generations are not as important as the process that lies in the story, the history behind them: all that risk, hope in the new, suffering and delight in God's presence, as well as the less commendable aspects of human behaviour. What this pilgrimage with the Gospel does is place you alongside the Gospel. So, you begin to know Jesus, not just admire Him or believe Him. This knowing is about falling in love with God in Christ who is in Abraham, the one who risks leaving his home to create the new community. For Francis, this 'pilgrimage' is about leaving home. Using this imaginary story is about taking a risk to follow him, as many did when they followed Abraham as he left home. You will do some looking; looking in hope of fulfilment of God's promise of unity: to realise that you are 'at one' with the Divine – the realisation of Love. You will do some suffering. There is the suffering of the great ones in the development of Israel, leading to the suffering of God Himself – Jesus Christ. God is present in your history intimately. So you might consider getting to know your history 'in God' with a little more attention, so that you can participate in the journey with creativity and healing. So here's the sentence for you to 'dwell' on for a few moments.

Lead me, Christ, into a deeper Knowledge of Your Way!

THE EXERCISE

You're part of a race with all its memories, many of which are forgotten and lie deep in the unconsciousness. This meditation doesn't happen in isolation although you may be alone at this moment. Jesus comes to you from a vast array of human beings throughout history. The wonder of that is almost numbing. The meditation sentence implies a trusting attitude that you'll perceive Jesus deeply in you, as he hungers to be 'here' for you right now in the Gospel. Don't be hindered by a false sense of inadequacy. It may be that following your praying with Matthew through each sentence you will want to know more, understand more. Allow this sentence to 'take you by the hand' and lead you to your intimate friendship with Jesus among the staggering myriad of followers known and unknown. Matthew's list only scratches the surface! Whose names would you write inside your copy of the Gospel? Only move on, when you feel ready and when you have the time and space.

- - -

2.

THE PILGRIMAGE

Just after setting out to walk, we notice a young couple sitting huddled by the side of the road. It becomes clear that the young woman was heavily pregnant and in pain. As if he knows what he's talking about, Francis is direct with her. "Just breathe deeply, lady!" "What do you think I am doing?" she snaps impatiently. Francis turns to me and with a huge smile across his face, shouts with glee, "What a start to our pilgrimage. A birth!" And so, a birth - and Francis did know what to do! What am I doing with this man?

Read the section: Matthew 1. 18-25.

THE REFLECTION

The emphasis on the Holy Spirit is fundamental as it is the presence of the activity of God at the very roots of all life, of all living, no matter where, when or how - even at the side of a road. The Spirit is the 'name' given to the means by which all human life comes into being. Jesus' birth is unique, but it isn't inaccessible. All births are unique. The birth of Jesus draws attention to God's absolute involvement in Creation. The Spirit is the creativity of God who constantly is in the 'new' – firmly in the history and life-system of the universe. This birth is now – here – with you.

I would realise the Life of Christ within me through the Holy Spirit!

THE EXERCISE

This meditation sentence demands self-acceptance, the love of yourself and, of course, patience. Realising the depth of the Spirit within you is a lifetime's process. As your development as a unique human takes time. So, slow down and take time with this sentence. By practicing this prayer at the beginning of the day when you are alert and expectant, you are cooperating with the vibrancy of God within, who wants to bring to birth in you the Christ. It's a 'wake up' call, gentle and strong.

- - -

CHAPTER TWO – MATTHEW 2

3.

THE PILGRIMAGE

Each night of the pilgrimage so far, we sleep more or less in the open. There's been the occasional barn or derelict cottage. Sleep has been fitful; not helped by Francis getting up to relieve himself several times during the night and groaning in the process. "Do you have to grunt and groan, waking me up. Don't tell me this is going to happen every night?" "What if it does?" is Francis' less than comforting reply. "Or was that him praying?" "So what if it was," he replies even more comfortingly. He insists that we get up early, no matter how I'm feeling. "If God is to be All for you, then greet him with your all before anything else." I want to go home!

Read the section: Matthew 2:1-12

THE REFLECTION

In Franciscan 'iconography', the child Jesus is shown with his arms stretched, being supported by his Mother, his feet are placed on his Mother's knees. This is an open, loving posture, but it is also anticipates his crucifixion. This openness and powerlessness puts a question mark over the powerful. The mystery of Jesus' paradoxical power, to those who follow him, is revealed where justice and well-being has been cut-off. The powerful wise men visited this powerless child with their priceless gifts. Wisdom knows where to look for the Love of God. In their approach to the child Jesus, they throw away their power.

Christ the King, let me find You in the small and vulnerable and bring my gift.

THE EXERCISE

The wisdom to see Christ in the alienated comes from prayer. Without it, union with God is only talking about an idea. The difficulty is that the small and vulnerable are easily missed. More often, they are ignored. Busy-ness and pre-occupation, however, are stilled by entering deeply into prayer. Allow yourself to 'look at' Jesus, the child. Let the imagination run free. Then look at where you see this fragility, this smallness in your own daily living. The gift you have, may not amount to much in your eyes. It may, for the vulnerable, on the other hand, be life-giving. Now, imagine yourself as Jesus the child.

- - -

4.

THE PILGRIMAGE

I can't help wondering what's happened to the young pregnant lady. Has the baby been born well and strong? "What do you think Francis? You seem to know about these things. Will the baby thrive?" Without any hesitation, he replies' "The baby will be well. As usual, it's the parents I'm concerned about. Wisdom lies deep in the newly born. The question is, however, will that wisdom be given the space and freedom to flourish?"

Read the section: Matthew 2:13-18

THE REFLECTION

If the child Jesus had not been taken to Egypt, maybe his death would have happenedin this early part of the Gospel narrative, and those 'innocents' would, almost certainly, not have been slaughtered. At what price, Jesus' survival? The apostles also lost their lives in brutal circumstances. Hard though it is, we are asked to focus on Jesus Christ in the middle of those circumstances, making The Way of Love through history including hell itself. Jesus' parents waited in Egypt for God's guidance. Those who follow Christ are such as the parents of Christ: people of hope, who have the courage to wait, despite apparent hopelessness. Where's he gone now?

Grant me obedience and determination to wait on Your Will being awakened within me.

THE EXERCISE

One of the challenges in silence and prayer can be a sense of hopelessness, feeling it's a waste of time. In the sentence, the word 'obedience' is not about subservience, being a door-mat. Obedience is the demand of the absolute goodness of God that waits on your love. Your circumstances, no matter how dark they may be, are where Jesus is. It may be in the middle of the darkness that the Love of God is made known deep within you. So, wait.

- - -

5.

THE PILGRIMAGE

Several times, I've commented to Francis that I haven't come across what some called 'holy places'. He looks at me with a knowing smile. "Every pilgrimage is about sacred, holy places, some will be noticed and most go unnoticed," comes Francis edgy comment, with that look that suggests I haven't noticed. After a break for water, Francis kneels in the middle of the track. "What are you doing, Francis? This isn't a holy place!", I add scorn- fully. "Be quiet! Sacred places are constantly revealed to you. Kneel! The track is holy!" Resentfully, I kneel. What is he talking about?

Read the section: Matthew 2:19-23

THE REFLECTION

At the beginning of the Gospel, the Holy Family make their way into the region of Galilee. At the end of the Gospel, the angel tells those who are looking for Jesus to go to Galilee to meet and greet the risen Christ. It's in Galilee that the disciples first encounter Jesus. The sacredness of place comes from the significance of the event experienced. Revisiting holy places is a deep human desire. What's more, Galilee gave some safety, as Jesus was still under threat. Picasso, the great Spanish artist, remembered being held firmly and lovingly in the arms of his grandfather in a terrifying earthquake: love and tenderness in the middle of trauma. The memory of that experience he maintained added strength to his artistic creativity. The place of such love, a Galilee moment, is sacred and creative.

I thank You for Your Holiness in the places You have led me.

THE EXERCISE

Recollect a place where you have experienced an important personal event. Perhaps it's difficult to describe, but take time to relive the event, with all your senses. A recollection of the sacredness of place; a 'Galilee' moment. It may be significant to you because of darkness in your life. As you make this pilgrimage and eventually come to its completion, this Galilee moment, you'll see becomes even more significant. Jesus, in the depths, is bringing deep healing and strength. Keep a brief note of your prayer experience.

- - -

CHAPTER THREE – MATTHEW 3

6.

THE PILGRIMAGE

I notice that my breathing gets shallower as the day's walking progresses. I'm tired already. "Oh alright then!", he grunts impatiently, "We'll have a rest. So lie down and look up at the sky." We're at the side of the path. "But the grass is damp". He pays no attention. but lies down giving me instructions of how to breathe gently and in the same rhythm as him. "Now, when you stand up, keep that gentle breathing pattern going". "I suppose you're going to tell me that this breathing is an important part of praying," I ask rather unenthusiastically. "It's what prayer IS. Trusting." Read the section.

Read the section: Matthew 3:1-12

THE REFLECTION

John the Baptist states clearly that the Kingdom of God is at hand. The Kingdom [or better 'The Reign'] is the process by which those in Christ are brought into the unity and love of God. It's at hand and yet it's not yet. Baptism is being turned towards readiness for that Kingdom. Repentance, which is a turning towards God, is demanding because it involves letting go of resistance.

When I begin to let this happen, I experience a little of what the love of God is – what the Gospels call the Kingdom of God – God 'reigning' in me.

Turn to me and I will transform your living for My Loving.

THE EXERCISE

To let go of that which gets in the way of the Love of God, the attitude of trust in prayer must be practiced. With it goes repentance: What is replacing the Love of God in my life? Simply observe and don't be harsh on yourself. God certainly won't be! God now comes to you and gently turns you towards the way of love and loving. When you come out of this prayer, you may have someone in mind who can help you to talk through what arose in your prayer.

- - -

7.

THE PILGRIMAGE

Having walked through a small village, we sit beside a muddy pond, with unmentionables floating on the surface. I turn to Francis, "Can't we go to another spot to eat our bread and fruit?" "Look carefully and tell me what you see." "Come on, Francis, do I have to describe it?" He smiles. "Yes, even in this, we also perceive the presence of the Beloved." "Oh! really?", I add sarcastically. As we walk away, the air cleared of the fetid smell. Smelly rubbish and God? And why did Francis use the word Beloved?

Read the section: Matthew 3:13-17

THE REFLECTION

'This is My Son...' These are words spoken in this moment to you, male or female! Be with John the Baptist and experience what he experienced. Acceptance, surprise, apprehension, delight...right in the middle of the experience of repentance. Jesus enters into the heart of human lostness, even the void that feels like alienation from God. The deep entering of Jesus into me, brings the forgiveness of God. The Spirit is the active means of this experience that continues right through to praying. "This is My Son" in my praying.

Holy Spirit, open my heart that I may know that This is Your Beloved in the work of forgiveness!

EXERCISE

Notice the work of the Spirit in this passage. Be there with Christ as the Spirit descends on Him. Hear the words 'This is My Son' spoken to you. What do you see? What do you feel? Respond from your gut. With such simple experiences, what's your response? 'With whom I am well pleased' expresses the delight of being in an intimate union of self-giving love. You too are precious. Like Christ, God delights in you. Enjoy this praying.

- - -

CHAPTER FOUR – MATTHEW 4

8.

THE PILGRIMAGE

I've noticed already how important finding time to pray is for Francis. Perhaps I'll catch the discipline behind his 'slip-stream'. Today, as he stopped for half an hour, I just couldn't be bothered. With this attitude, I notice that my ability to discover the presence of God around me diminishes. "What did you mean by the word "Beloved"? Who are you talking about?" "Ah! It's a way of describing being intimate with God, being intimate with Jesus, in the same way you describe someone with whom you are in love." "In love with God?" is my dismissive question. "An even deeper more intense love!" He walks on, with a determined look. There are moments already on this pilgrimage when I can't be bothered with spirituality and praying. "Can't I just be ordinary?" "Yes," replies Francis. "Really ordinary. Have the humility to allow yourself to be loved by the Beloved. That's ordinary enough for anyone!". "But I don't feel this love. I feel dry and empty." "Even better," smiles Francis. "The desert meeting with love!"

Read the section.: Matthew 4:1-11

REFLECTION

Faith is acknowledging effectively that I'm in union with God even if I've no sense of what that means. There's no security in the desert. The danger to faith is the desire for security – protection for suffering and fear. Fear also is the basis for the desire to have influence over others. The desert simplifies choices: to react out of fear or out of love. Love is the activity of God where there is insecurity. The Spirit leads Jesus into insecurity not as a test but to strengthen His obedience to God.

Let the Holy Spirit lead you to live by My Grace, My Simplicity and My Freedom.

EXERCISE

The Spirit acts in you as you desire to pray at depth. So, use the sentence to still you, perhaps, take you into a place of insecurity and uncertainty. Be in the desert with Jesus. Your desires for security, protection, and influence may reveal uncomfortable facets of your personality. Don't judge or analyse yourself. Just notice them. Let them be. Tell them "to get behind you", even if only for a while! You are with and in the simplicity of prayer. So, you are free to react just as you feel.

- - -

9.

THE PILGRIMAGE

Francis is very demanding! But, I have to admit, he's helping me to create space within me. This morning we're sitting outside a barn, where we had been sheltering from the rain. Francis starts to put on that serious, teaching look. "Those dedicated to the Christ-like life, are conscious of how they can 'block out the light'." "I'm not sure what you mean. Give me an example." "Well. One of the great skills in drama is that actors and singers will make sure that they don't get in the way of the art; the story, the atmosphere." Francis, I've noticed, makes sure that he doesn't get in the way of Christ's presence on the pilgrimage, and by his attention, he urges me to watch more, to practice silence in order to let the pilgrimage be made with Jesus and let go that incessant, insatiable desire for achievement.

Read the section: Matthew 4.12-17

REFLECTION

Matthias Grünewald's painting of the Crucifixion shows John the Baptist pointing towards Christ with the Scriptures open at the words: 'I must decrease so that he may increase.' John followed in the footsteps of Elijah, one of the great Old Testament prophets, whose job it was to expose the hearts, the motivation of humanity. The Hebrew Scriptures are a vital means of understanding the roots of Christ's presence in history. John saw into the heart of Christ and so prepared the way for Him. He didn't get in the way. To know Christ is to see, watch where the lost are found and recovered and the hungry fed. I'm a follower of The Way.

I thank You for all those who have brought me insight into Your Presence.

EXERCISE

Maybe you might take some notes. John the Baptist is pointing you in the direction of Jesus. Let John take you to Jesus personally and intimately. Now, let the Spirit show you those in your own story who have pointed you to Christ's presence. Write their names. They may be people you know, have met briefly or you've read or heard about: living now or in the past. See them in front of you and thank God for them. They've got out of your way.

- - -

10.

PILGRIMAGE

"Pilgrimages are about the present moment, here, now, what's going on." "Oh. Come on Francis! Be realistic, it's cold and I'm soaked, that's what's going on!" "Quite! So I'll just pull my hood over my head, and read these verses of Matthew. Oh! Then I'll take some time just walking in some kind of rhythm, weather permitting, and praying with my breath and my footsteps...." "But, you've got your hood over your head and you won't see where you're going." "You walk behind me and tell me when I'm about to walk into a tree and trip over a boulder." Well, alright then!" I moan.

Read the section: Matthew 4.18-22

REFLECTION

Attractive and hazardous. No caution. Instantaneous obedience to following Christ. There are no requests for security. Perhaps this setting out with Francis is a taste of insecurity. It's a waste of time speculating on the motive behind this following of Jesus. Why did those ordinary folk follow Jesus? God's demand and the resulting obedient, single-hearted response in the Gospel seem to be absolute. Well, God is described by one great 20th century mystic as Absolute Goodness. The fishermen's nets are vital, even for the local economy, but Jesus' demand puts a question mark over all enterprises, including sensible ones. Any attempt to make this passage easier, doesn't work. When Love calls there is an option – Yes or No!

I would receive Your Gifts of Truth and Freedom that I may follow You.

EXERCISE

Obedience to God, following Jesus, isn't heroism. It's the simple service of the lowliest, where God is, without being noticed. Loving the humdrum with the best of you. So what gets in the way of this? Let Jesus drop into your heart the words: "Follow me!" with your response as in the sentence. Don't worry about outcomes or false expectations. Just listen and watch in prayer and the more that that happens the more you will respond with the only response possible for you. Amen – Yes!!

- - -

11.

PILGRIMAGE

There are moments in these early stages with Francis when I ask myself: do I really want to carry on this pilgrimage? When feeling fed up, I just want to turn off the path. Francis walks behind me, but not to poke me; not to tell me what to feel or do. He says the simplest of things: "I can't feel what you feel, my friend, but Jesus walks with us?" He notices that I'm not convinced. "Well, we'll stop. Have some water; open your gospel and try this meditation and then have a nap! You'll remember why you are on this pilgrimage." Mmmm?

Read the section: Matthew 4.23-25

REFLECTION

Being brought to Jesus. Desperate people seem to have the attention on them. However, it's easy to miss those that brought the sick to Jesus. 'Being brought' carries on the process begun in John the Baptist. He points away from himself to Jesus. The people who bring the sick to Jesus point away from themselves. They know to whom they are 'pointing'. The demand of the Gospel is to know Jesus so that I can point to Him, wherever hope is given in poverty, disease and among the hopeless. And where Jesus is, God is.

Through the Spirit within me, let me bring others to Your Hope and Your Health

EXERCISE

When someone brings you to meet someone, you're dependent. That dependence brings an ease. St Teresa of Avila, the Spanish Mystic, was in internal turmoil for years and she allowed herself to be carried spiritually by others. They didn't only pray for her, but instead of her. Who has brought you to places where you can relax and feel free? Maybe it's someone who has brought you healing, forgiveness or well – someone who loves you. See and feel the person bringing you to Jesus. They haven't got in the way. Who have you brought, carried to a place of peace and health? Is there someone you can bring now in your imagination? Don't get in the way of the Love of God.

- - -

CHAPTER FIVE – MATTHEW 5

12.

THE PILGRIMAGE

I have just felt Francis' arm around my shoulder. "I've noticed that you're not really 'present' as you walk." As he holds me, I begin to sense his 'passion'; his single-heartedness in Jesus. A simple touch from him is a beatitude. "What I want you to do, Francis, is open your Gospel and read the Beatitudes to me. Let's sit on this rock. I'll close my eyes, eat some cheese ~~you~~ and listen to you. Then I'll repeat what you have read, verse by verse, as you eat some cheese". "But wait a minute! Will there be any cheese left by then?" I reply rather cheekily, "So who's not living in the present moment now?" At least, he laughed. Here's hoping!

Read the section: Matthew 5.1-12

REFLECTION

The trouble about the title The Beatitudes is that it can easily feel as if they're a collection of aphorisms, pithy, memorable sayings, whereas they're active processes. Present moment, waking up guidance. 'Beatitude' is better as a verb. God is 'beatituding'. These verses are, in effect, eight ways of being brought into God. The deeper this unity, the deeper you are blessing; the deeper you 'beatitude' those around you. But the temptation is to turn your living with God into a project. Jesus' eight 'verb' ways enter into the whole of my life. Integration happens when I see my praying and my living affect each other and become one. In fact, they're already one.

Let the poverty of your heart draw you into My Way!

EXERCISE

Try remembering the Beatitudes, the 'eight ways' of blessing 'by heart'. To do so is to allow them to enter deeply into you. There is a better chance then that they become part of you. Another approach to praying this passage is to focus on just one of the 'ways', as the sentence above illustrates. Poverty, for example, isn't only a word that suggests a lack; it's a willingness to be empty in order to receive. One of the methods of letting yourself experience this spiritual emptying is to imagine that Christ's eyes are fixed on you as he speaks the words of the Beatitudes. So doing, you will recognise the poverty in you that will open the way for the gaze of Christ.

- - -

13.

PILGRIMAGE

Sometimes it seems that I am just putting one foot in front of the other and waiting for the next glass of wine! And where are we going? Francis seems constantly to be on the look-out, as if he's expecting someone to join us; or to be seeing always something significant, making his own walking seem more attentive than mine. Is this something to do with his awareness of Christ? Perhaps. Sometimes I notice him smiling and shaking his head. I asked him what he was thinking. "I'm saying to myself: Waken up, look and listen!" I suppose he is speaking to me as well! "Oh! And smell, touch and taste."

Read the section: Matthew 5.13-16

REFLECTION

So, good works, perhaps, but Jesus is clear that they are not about me or about Him, but about praising, pointing deep gratitude to 'your Father'. So, the good works point away from me and to God. Again, I'm reminded of John the Baptist pointing to Jesus and not getting in the way. He was clear about his task. Now, I've a particular task I am asked to do for God. And so do you! I may be unclear what it is, but someone close to me might know. But, the light of Jesus shines through me just as I am: the one Jesus loves! And I may not have a clue what I'm doing, if anything. The rest is the work of the Spirit of God. That involves trust. That's hard.

I would know Your Light within me to be a source of hope to those in darkness.

EXERCISE

What's the work that Christ wants of you? Ask Him! But be careful! You may be doing that work and you're not aware of it. Guilt exacerbated by what you think you're not doing is destructive in prayer as well as in your living. Now imagine someone you admire (a famous person in history for example) asking you to work for her or him. Something immediate, practical. What do you imagine that to be? Don't think too hard – just let your imagination run. Now imagine Christ asking you to 'help' him. Let yourself be free and stay with the images and feelings. After you have left your meditation, note down any reactions, images or feelings.

- - -

14.

PILGRIMAGE

For days, I've avoided meditation. All I seem to do when I pray is stare and meander about in my mind and imagination. Prayer might be described for me as the chronicle of a chaotic mind. "Who told you that your inner life is chaos?" Francis asks, just before going to sleep. I can see him smile out of the corner of my eye. Sometimes smiles are infuriating. He doesn't have to say anything. Not that this exchange is about my guilt: those 'oughts' and 'shoulds'. He is simply making me aware of my inclination to avoid, to resist. "Just pray by breathing easily, rhythmically and gently... and even smile." "At what?" "At who!" He laughed. "Oh. And chaotic minds are probably more interesting!" he adds enigmatically.

Read the section: Matthew 5.17-19

REFLECTION

This section is about balance. On the one hand, the 'Law' is about obedience to God and the sacred instructions as to how to be obedient. A central part of Moses' Law was, of course, the Ten Commandments. On the other hand, the 'Prophets' were those who had insight into the Revelation of God in their midst – God among us – Immanuel. Nothing must get in the way of the

Love of God. The prophets are those who point the ways in which we avoid or evade that obedience.

Let My Love of You draw you into My Way and My Truth!

EXERCISE

Remembering the Ten Commandments by heart is also worth while. They may seem bald and even possessive. But they point to life in God that mustn't be blocked by attitudes that negate that life. Prayer is the beginning of this obedience: the discipline of your life fully attentive to God's love in history, including your own intimate history. The sentence is a way of having the depths of our consciousness disciplined, 'drawn' into God. When you are passionate, in love, you're being obedient to that passion and love which you're experiencing. Give sometime to thinking and praying of examples of obedience which you have admired and which have challenged you.

- - -

15.

PILGRIMAGE

We stop to buy food and fill our bottles. I then sit on a bench in the square just staring at nothing. Or am I? Francis sits beside me. "You're carrying something in your heart. Do you want to tell me about it?" He looks intently into my eyes. So, with a sigh, I tell him that I'd hoped that the pilgrimage would be an opportunity to deal with a deep hurt in me. Instead of that it has grown worse.

Read the section: Matthew 5:20-26

REFLECTION

There's a baldness to how the Gospel portrays Jesus in his teaching about reconciliation. The first task of all relationships is reconciliation and that means being open in how I've failed in it. Forgiveness is so difficult because hurt can be deep in the memory. To work on forgiveness has psychological, ethical and physical value. However, reconciliation is a living out of the activity of God's forgiveness. The hurt is used, transfigured by God, not forgotten. Putting it bluntly, God demands forgiveness. And forgiveness is theological: the heart of God in Christ. To be reconciled is to cooperate with the process of God's work. It's not about making me feel better. I'm summoned by Love to live beyond myself. To forgive involves my realisation of the Spirit of God reconciling within me.

Let the Spirit of God deepen my desire for Your Reconciliation!

EXERCISE

Remembering someone I've hurt, can bring feelings of guilt and even resentment. Despite my remorse, I may have the residue of feeling that the person I hurt was asking for it, deserved it. Maybe I've spoken words of forgiveness, but the feelings lie beyond words and can last a life-time. Meeting the person seems too much. The reconciliation of God comes to heal and transfigure my feelings. So see, look at the person or persons you've hurt or who may have hurt you. Let them pass before you without analysing. Then use the meditation sentence. If feelings do arise, don't force them away. Simply acknowledge them. Holding a cross can draw you away from unnecessarily negative feelings about yourself or anyone else. Writing down the feelings can help you begin to let them go. Give your attention to the sentence.

- - -

16.

PILGRIMAGE

Francis listens. He watches. It seems he is here for me, or whoever he is with. My difficulty is trust, despite my sense that, inexplicably, he holds me in his heart. Today, I notice that as he leans across a fence to talk to a farmer feeding his cattle, he's attentive to him as well. Yes, I'm jealous! Francis notices. "You have that pinched look to your face." I daren't admit to him that I want his company on this pilgrimage just for me. "Oh. It's nothing." I add rather helplessly. "It'll pass." "Do you want to walk this pilgrimage on your own?" I'm now hurting. Francis doesn't really understand; at least some of the time. I recognise that I want Jesus to be for me too and shaped accordingly!

Read the section: Matthew 5:27-32

REFLECTION

Lust and adultery are not to be taken as central. There was among some religious people who heard Matthew's Gospel, strong expectation of the arrival of a Kingdom. Anything that gets in the way of the centrality of God, might lead to a lack of preparedness for, an urgency about the coming of the Kingdom. Sexuality itself, its enjoyment doesn't get in the way. It's a gift. However, the desire to possess the one I long for, that's where the difficulty begins. In fact, that which I want to possess is simply the image of myself in the other. Being too attached to the one whom I desire, causes freedom in love to be lost. Being 'cast into hell' is a poetic description of what it is to be separated from love; separated from the freedom that is the non-possessiveness of the Love of God.

Let your heart be open to the Love of My Holiness.

EXERCISE

There's the fear that if I choose the Love of God over possessing what I desire: sex or otherwise, I might be left with nothing. So ask for the gift of being open to all the possibilities of freedom and not possession. You may then be an instrument of freedom for others. You don't need to possess anyone. In any case, you can't! You're free. Holiness is nothing other than the freedom of God. This meditation can bring pain as in the silence you're bound to encounter the possessiveness that can strangle freedom. Staying with the sentence will help you to move beyond the choke of possessiveness to the freedom of God, just a little.

- - -

17.

PILGRIMAGE

Francis talks to two men sitting on a wall, holding empty bottles of cheap wine. "You don't look as if you're enjoying yourself", he observes. But they ignore him, as he listens to their abusive attitudes, thinly disguising the terror in their hearts. From his rucksack, he takes out his bread and his flask, gives it to them and walks away, having laid his hand on each of their heads: a simple blessing. "But what are you going to eat?", I asked him, anxiously. "Well, there's your packed lunch, isn't there?" "Thank you very much!", I sneer.

Read the section: Matthew 5:33-37

REFLECTION

The legal world depends on swearing and so do international politics: treaties, vows or oaths, no matter how many of them may be broken. Because of my human insecurity, when I desire a relationship with someone, I want that person to be bound to me. All this arises from my basic desire for security, which can then be distorted into my wanting power over you. But Christianity has at its heart that strange paradox of wisdom and strength in insecurity. Jesus demands simplicity because relationships in the Kingdom are simple and free: 'yes' or 'no'.

Here and now, I am asked to begin practicing a kind of insecurity: the simplicity of God.

That my words and actions may reflect the simplicity of Your Truth within me.

EXERCISE

Prayer brings with it insecurity. Don't expect prayer to be primarily about comfort and security. After all, when you pray, you may only be negotiating with the four walls and the furniture around you. So, there's courage in praying, because there's nothing to possess, but a unique freedom in praying in the presence of the Love of God. You might find it helpful to have someone who'll help you discern where your securities and insecurities lie. The sentence above is about becoming detached from possessiveness, the foolishness of security. In the depth of your heart, you are enfolded in a love that is beyond any allegiance.

- - -

18.

PILGRIMAGE

Several times a day, I stop someone who passes us to ask for news on the war we've heard about. Francis doesn't seem to be that concerned. And yet, he's aware of what's going on. "The key is knowing what lies at the roots of conflict: decisions made out of fear, not love." He realises I'm frightened by the news. What's more, he sees even more poignantly that my fear is for myself. "What will happen to me?" is my prevailing question, which I don't admit, of course. "I know,'" said Francis. "Think of this. Acknowledging your fear is enough experience of the Light of Christ to be going on with." And I didn't even open my mouth!

Read the section: Matthew 5:38-42

REFLECTION

Throughout the day, the amount of resisting I do, sometimes shames me! And here Jesus is demanding: Don't resist! The focus of the Sermon on the Mount, remember, is God. In God, life and death are part of the way I'm created. I can find God in all of creation without exception, hard though that may be. However, there's the disturbing defensiveness in me that arises from my fear. To practice non-resistance is to live with faith in non-violence that God enables, even against the flow of pragmatism. Tragically, it may be that circumstances force me to be and do otherwise. That is why all aggression, even if argued ethically necessary, is a matter of confession and repentance. Aggression that is accompanied with triumph, perhaps, must be challenged.

My Grace brings healing to the roots of your fear.

EXERCISE

God is absolute good, the holy, wholly Other. 'Holiness' is beyond my understanding. In Jesus, that otherness is intimately present to me. Try recalling someone with whom you may have had conflict, or maybe still have. Don't spend time with feelings of aggression because that'll disturb your praying, but simply notice them without analysis or judgement. Invite Jesus to be with you, to enter deeply into your fears. There's no instant panacea, but a life-time's faithfulness to peace-making, peace-keeping and reconciliation.

- - -

19.

PILGRIMAGE

Francis is leaning over my shoulder, as we read a notice on a wall about being careful of 'The Enemy'. He seems sad as we read on: 'Enemy forces massing...' 'Borders...' 'Boundaries...' Noticing fear in my eyes, Francis doesn't need to say anything. The fear and the dislike, the borders are in me! "Alright, Francis. I recognise that enmity is in me. What do I do about it to change?" "Do you want to change? Try not changing, but just accepting that all these negatives are in you. Then wait, trust."

Read the section: Matthew 5:43-48

REFLECTION

Love your enemies. This is no soft or polite suggestion. It's a 'Kingdom' demand on communities as well as individuals. There's little if any concession to pragmatism; no compromise with political realism. Along with most other Gospel demands, it seems impossible! However, the Gospels are read from the 'other side' of the Crucifixion and Resurrection, as it were, where what is impossible becomes experience for Christians. From the perspective of the Gospel experience, that experience is of the heart. To transform attitudes about 'enemies' is a demand. In following Jesus, I'm to love my enemies and am given 'power' to fulfil that call. This will definitely lead to deep unpopularity at worst and at best a tolerant smile at impracticality. Indeed, it is a miniature taste of the crucifixion.

Open the dark corners of your heart. Acknowledge your fears. Be released of your enmities.

EXERCISE

Hatred within me and from me only happens where there's been love. It isn't dislike, but the fear that comes as a result of my alienation from those I've loved and have loved me. What is so hard is to take responsibility for fear and enmity. It's easier to project hatred on to someone else, another country, a political figure - 'demonising' that person. Tyrannies are born and thrive where that projection becomes the focus for a whole people. With this sentence, slowly begin to have peace in yourself that may, in the Grace of God, affect those from whom you may be alienated.

- - -

CHAPTER SIX – MATTHEW 6

20.

PILGRIMAGE

We've some miles to go until we arrive at our lodgings. It's dark. Where's Francis? I retrace my steps. The wind and rain is driving against my face. "What are you doing, Francis?" I shout angrily but with relief. No reply. He's sitting by a fence with the hood over his head. "Sit beside me and shut up!" His hands are buried in the folds of his cloak. "Watch!" he shouts. "Watch what?" Then I realise. He's gone 'into his inner room'. Gradually over the days and weeks, I would come to know that this is a priority for him.

Read the section: Matthew 6:1-6

REFLECTION

Being sometimes too attached to people, circumstances and, yes, things, means that I don't listen or look as I might. Being detached from all these isn't easy, but it's being aware of what's going on around me; being engaged with people and circumstances creatively. Detachment isn't about being aloof and distant, but it creates space within me in order to listen to God in all things. Praying is the practice of this detachment. By going into my 'inner room', I let go the desire to seem spiritual or being apprehensive about, or drawn to others around me. A 'secret' corner for prayer helps detachment and simplicity.

I would receive the inner gift of attention to Your Holiness.

EXERCISE

Create a little corner with a candle, a favourite book on praying; of prayers, perhaps a bible, a crucifix, an icon. If you're in a room by yourself, close the curtains and turn off the radio and telephone. The silence is a gift of God. Practice stillness. No one is watching you, scrutinising you. So picture Christ sitting or kneeling beside you, still and being attentive to 'Abba'. Try this for 20 minutes.

- - -

21.

PILGRIMAGE

Moaning to Francis, I tell him that going up and down on this uneven path is tiring. "I'm hungry", he replies sharply. At last: A stop! Passing through a little town, we come across a Church that has its doors locked. The name of the priest is pinned to the door. So we go to the Priest's little house and he invites us in. There are five or six folk around a little table; an old glass and a plate with a loaf of bread. "Why not in the Church?" "Because", says the priest, "the roof is leaking." Francis enters into silence and it's catching. "Teach us to pray", one of them whispers. The priest adds, "And, while you're at it, teach me to pray too!" Holiness speaks in silences clearly!

Read the section: Matthew 6:7-15

REFLECTION

Prayer isn't an isolated practice. Jesus teaches you to pray by giving himself. The Lord's Prayer after all, includes: 'Give us this day our daily bread'. Prayer feeds because the Eucharist feeds. The first two words of the Lord's Prayer are 'Our Father', not 'My Father'. So even when you are apparently praying by yourself, you are with the Body of Christ as that Body is experienced throughout history, both in the living and in the departed, most of whom you don't know. You are with the prophets, the saints and all the unknown ones who have prayed this prayer.

Come Source of all and draw me into the Unity of Your Son's Body.

EXERCISE

'Our Father' said, prayed in my heart is an acknowledgement that I'm already with others, no matter
where I happen to be. Humanity and indeed all of creation are in fact united. There's a tragedy in not
realising this unity. It's already here! Pray that you are
one with those around you and beyond. You've learnt,
probably, to see everybody and everything around you
as separate from you, except, perhaps, the people and
the things that you desire. This sentence takes you into
a deeper place to where the Spirit of God brings Unity.
What's more, it's the essential work of intercession.

- - -

22.

PILGRIMAGE

Francis is fasting and he's asked me to join him. He has
water with him and simple biscuits."Must I?" I ask
grumpily. He simply looks at me as if it's a waste of
time answering my question. Resting on a guesthouse
bunk, Francis stares at the ceiling. "There on the ceiling
is a support that goes across the room. At right angles
are the wooden slats of the ceiling. I'm using that as a
cross to help me pray and, believe it or not, 'be' with
the fasting, even the starving Jesus.' "No walking on the

pilgrimage today, but attention, in stillness and silence, to those who are famished", he says with a kind of gentle assurance. "But how does this help the famished?" He puts his finger to his lips. Maybe the pilgrimage is for others.

Read the section: Matthew 6:16-21

REFLECTION

The spiritual life, I keep reminding myself, isn't about self-improvement. Personal physical or emotional well-being is experienced in the Christian community to which you belong and to which you're accountable, in order to work for the breaking-in of God's love around you. The practice of fasting, therefore, isn't about dieting; more of a resisting a particular desire in order to be open to God's desire for you. That's the treasure that is incorruptible. Carefully managed fasting heightens the awareness in prayer to obedience to Christ.

Persevere in your love for Me within your heart and in your attitudes.

EXERCISE

These sentences are to be used in silence and stillness, taking them into your heart so that it's in rhythm with your breathing; your living. So, to practice fasting, don't just observe your eating habits. In your prayer, see what other desires for possession and consumption you have. Fasting is not so much whether you could have used your money more effectively for others, important though that may be. Nor is it a matter of whether you indulge yourself on food and drink. Delight in having a good meal in company is life-giving. The question is: Do these get in the way of God's desire for you? Seek experienced advice on fasting particularly as to what the real motivation might be. And your health circumstances must be watched. A spiritual director will help.

- - -

23.

THE PILGRIMAGE

A young woman has joined us today. She's carrying next to nothing on her back, seemingly intent on little else but getting to the end of her pilgrimage. I approach her tentatively, "Tell me how you manage with so little." Francis shakes his head, "Just watch, listen to her in her silence and you'll be invited into her spiritual journey." I'm feeling humiliated again by Francis' slight reprimand. "What's wrong with asking her a few questions? I'm fascinated." Francis reply is even more difficult to take. "Yes, you're fascinated and that's your problem." My own pilgrimage might be a matter of self-fulfilment. "But I want her to experience some fulfilment," I reply plaintively. The young woman overhears me. "What's so important about fulfilment?" she smiles.

Read the section: Matthew 6:22-24

THE REFLECTION

Matthew's Gospel assumes that my attention is being re-focused, centred on God. The uncompromising demand in the Gospel is to be obedient to that centring on Jesus. By working at being attentive to God in prayer, my work and living become profoundly practical. Yes, my eyes are slaves of my desires and darkness prevails in my inner life. Attention to God brings freedom of heart and action, freedom not separate from those desires and darkness but through them.

Open the eyes of my heart that I may see You; my mind that I may perceive You; my hands that I may serve You.   *Bolt*

EXERCISE

Prayer is relationship to 'The Absolute Good'; my attention being drawn away from that which is not God. So look at the room or space you're in; become aware of your body, thoughts, emotions and feelings, imaginings. Become aware that they may be important but they are not God. It's coming to know God by the way of 'unknowing'. Once you have 'passed through' these aspects of your life, then allow the sentence above, or a small part of it, to hold your attention.

- - -

24.

THE PILGRIMAGE

Anxiety is a constant for me on the pilgrimage. My imagination and mind seems to be tuned to impending collapse or terror far away or something dreadful that might happen to us on the pilgrimage. The anxiety is about my life and my survival. "Francis, do you become afraid? Do you get frightened?" "Of course," he replies with that smile of his. "Being afraid is the way things actually are inside me. Facing the fear is essential for me but it demands courage and practice, leading me and you, if you practice, into the mystery of the God of Love."

Read the section: Matthew 6.25-33

THE REFLECTION

Perhaps the principal roots of anxiety are the threat of rejection, physical insecurity and the dread of death. They're all related, of course. To be rejected is a death. If I claim that I don't get frightened, frankly, I'm hiding. Of course, being afraid of something that may or may not happen in the future may beg questions, and can lead to mental health deterioration. However, guilt at being afraid is poisonous. The simple command "Do not worry. Do not be afraid." provides the opportunity to reassess where my trust is. If what I buy, wear, eat etc., is an attempt to protect myself from threat, then there's a question mark over what place my love in God has in the way I live and in the way I die.

Bring me into a deeper trust in You and transform the anxieties of my heart.

EXERCISE

In this prayer time, there's the opportunity, difficult though it may be, to face the guilt about being afraid. But anxiety must be handled with care, and perhaps if it has a grip on your life, you may benefit from professional advice and support. In deep praying, I become aware of the ways I protect myself from insecurity. There's no complete security but in the Love of God. The Love of God deepens your trust. But it's important for you, even if you feel reasonably strong, to share your anxieties with someone and to practice little acts of trust in the detail of your life.

- - -

CHAPTER SEVEN – MATTHEW 7

25.

THE PILGRIMAGE

A group of people sits beside me when I'm trying to have a nap on the dry grass. One of them asks me whether my life has been transformed by Christ. That doesn't feel like a question! Am I being preached at? Slowly, I get up to walk, hoping they won't go and bother Francis! He listens, watches them and says, "Thank you. But we need your help to build a little shelter for us all, because a storm is coming". They look at each other, put down their ruck-sacks and roll up their sleeves. The wind gathers speed after we finish, as we clutch mugs of milk. There's no more preaching, just work and the telling of stories.

Read the section: Matthew 7:1-5

THE REFLECTION

Praying gives less and less room to judgement of others. My judging you is about negative or destructive criticism. Positive criticism, however, is intent on something creative happening out of present circumstances. My judging tends to rise from my own fear of others. Finding God in all around me loosens the grip of my inclination to judge.

I would discern Your Hope in all around me.
        B O L D

EXERCISE

Silence increases my awareness of what is happening and who is around me. The simplicity of this silence is nothing other than the mystery of the presence of God and leads me into seeing others through that mystery: to see them as they really are. Look back over the last few hours and recollect the people you have been with. See them in the presence of Christ. Observe carefully. Take time. Then after a while, use the sentence to enable you even to see signs of hope in the most unlikely circumstance of your life.

- - -

26.

THE PILGRIMAGE

I adore simple food when on a walk; even more on this pilgrimage. "Can I use your knife to cut up this apple?" Francis asks. "Here. Have a piece", he suggests off-handedly. "I have my own", I answer. "Yes, I know". He then slices the apple carefully, applying maximum attention. He then hands me a slice. "Sacrament", he whispers in my ear with a cheeky smile.

Read the section: Matthew 7:6

THE REFLECTION

Here's a disturbing aspect of Jesus' unpredictable personality. All things are holy. I am to venerate all creatures, earwigs, cockroaches, daddy-longlegs and pied-wagtails. And what about the young woman sitting on a pavement playing her mouth-organ and begging. Money for drugs? Maybe. I'm to venerate her as well. Particular places and people are sacred, yes, but the sacred may be found in what seems the profane!

Let My Holiness go before all your words and actions.

EXERCISE

Wherever I pray, I'm in a sacred place and time. Maybe I've a favourite place to pray, a shrine that I love to visit or have heard of. Imagine such a place for yourself now. Be there. What makes it holy? You can go there any time in your imagination. Then use the sentence and linger in the atmosphere. As you leave your prayer ask God for the strength to 'be' that holiness in your words and actions. But remember, you will be the last to know!

- - -

27.

THE PILGRIMAGE

Francis is looking at a view along the path that winds along the coast. At the beauty of it, he begins to well up. 'I miss her terribly'. Francis gets a fright as he realises that I've overheard him. He's speaking of someone he has loved. He can see her face now. Why should this revelation of the private life of the saint surprise me? Francis is a passionate man, after all. He's chosen that other passionate path to leave home and walk with Matthew's Gospel and with me! I sensed that the tenderness of that love will remain with him. The pain of such a memory is also beautiful and is to be lived now. "I pray that I never lose the capacity of that love she taught me", he adds enigmatically.

Read the section: Matthew 7:7-12

THE REFLECTION

Everyone prays, whether they believe in God or not. It's a natural instinctive beseeching, begging and, yes, nagging. There's either the prayer of loving adoration: gazing at a loved-one, asking, pleading, even begging. When I'm frightened or lost, I beg. In front of a loved one, I know what to do and be, even if I fail. God loves me completely and without reserve or desert. What's commonly called 'Golden Rule' in these verses is about

God. How does God want me to treat others? When I love, and the one I love, that's God. Ubi caritas et amor, Deus ibi est. Where love in all its fullness is, there is God.

Be still and wait on the realisation of My Will within you.

EXERCISE

Ask God for what you want. Just be yourself. Write down your asking, your begging. Face it head on! Selfishness? You'll slowly realise what lies at the heart of your asking, which is the will of God. The object of your desire becomes more and more absorbed into your Love of God as your prayer deepens. The question you are asking may become more and more refined. Your questioning then becomes a longing for the divine.

- - -

28.

THE PILGRIMAGE

Francis has got me saying the breviary with him every day: the Church's discipline of Morning, Midday, Evening Prayer and Compline. As for the silent moments of prayer and meditation, I just don't know what to do, except imagine, dream of where the next meal is coming from. Yet another 'Magnificat' at the end of a long day's walking does not fill me with glee! "Come on Francis, I want to have that sense of closeness you seem to have with God". "Today", he said looking intently into my eyes, "You'll walk by yourself. You lead the way. You know the route. I'll follow two miles behind you." Was that an answer?

Read the section: Matthew 7:13-20

REFLECTION

Going through a narrow gate demands attention; to have courage and trust to enter the darkness of prayer. No one else can make that decision for me. It's the entry into the kingdom, the culture of God's love that is Christ-shaped: his death and resurrection. If I don't take responsibility for that attentive life by leaving it to the saints then there won't be enough room through the gate!

Be aware of My Truth and live in My Way each day.

EXERCISE

Guidance from others may be important as long as you recognise that you are the one who must work in prayer. Trying to be others because you admire them,

or because you ought to do what they suggest, is to con-
strict your way through the 'gate'. You've put on too
much weight! There is such a thing as spiritual obesity.
So, recollect someone who has given you important
guidance in prayer and the Christian life. Then let them
go and let your gaze be on Christ. This demands
courage, discipline and brings with it freedom and
strength.

- - -

29.

PILGRIMAGE

Sitting down by a huge log fire, Francis and I drink
some wine and eat some beef slices with bread.
Warming his hands, from his pocket, Francis pulls out
his copy of Matthew's Gospel, asking me to read the
next passage. Strangely, he then asks me whether I
regard him as having authority. Why would I otherwise
be on this pilgrimage? Silly man! But then he asks,
"What about your authority?" with a wry smile. I'm
embarrassed. Francis smiles and closes the Gospel,
falling silent by the fire. I fall asleep.

Read the section: Matthew 7:21-28

REFLECTION

Inner authority has two vital qualities: the inner life integrated with how I love, and freedom from the desire to manipulate or to impress. Christian language, however, is punctuated with words such as 'Lord! Lord!' The tragedy is that Jesus' 'Lordship' is so often misunderstood as dominance. The Latin roots of the word dominance is 'dominus' - lord. But, there's little point in talking about 'Jesus' if our lives don't have authority. Somebody who actually forgives; who actually lives for others, doesn't need to cultivate an authority. Christian authority is a gift of the Spirit within.

Deepen your silence in Me that you may practice My Loving.

EXERCISE

This meditation is about authority which allows you to be free of wanting to impress others including God! In a strange way, you may find yourself using the word 'God' or 'Jesus' less and less. Silence needs to be practiced so that you can realise the gift of the Spirit within which gives authority: authentic freedom to love without wanting to manipulate.

- - -

CHAPTER EIGHT – MATTHEW 8

30.

THE PILGRIMAGE

A gate into a field is lying off its hinges. Francis and I try to put it back. Laughing too much doesn't help. A boy in tears, we notice, is leaning against the dry stone wall. He'd tried to jump the gate earlier and hadn't made it. Francis looks at the leg, saying to the boy, "Look at that rabbit over there…" As the boy looks for the supposed rabbit, Francis gives his leg a quick pull. There's a scream. "It's not broken", he says. The boy looks at Francis in amazement and gets up gingerly to try his weight on his feet. When he looks up to say thank you, he realises that Francis has already left, with me standing staring.

Read the section: Matthew 8:1-4

REFLECTION

Why Jesus wanted no one to know about his healing miracle: curing a man of skin-disease, is puzzling. However, in this scene, I am drawn to God. But miracles attract adulation that detracts from Jesus who summons me to take responsibility for myself. God is as he is in Jesus. Christ who heals is also crucified, rubbing out celebrity. These healings are foretastes, trailers of a new culture of Love, drawing me to look beyond this moment in hope, not for a hero Christ, but within myself.

Awaken me to Thy Presence. Heal me in Thy Christ. Enliven me in Thy Spirit.

EXERCISE

Take responsibility for the God-given gift of hope and healing within you. Move into praying in order to leave and find the Love of God 'out there'. The sentence (or sentences!) are, at root, trinitarian: the Creativity of God present now (Father); the healing of Christ happening now (The Son) and the energy that keeps hope alive (The Spirit) expecting the fulfilment of love beyond this moment in the mystery of God. An interplay of intimacy and love at the very heart of the universe. Repeat the short phrases and then remain in silence.

- - -

31.

PILGRIMAGE

Francis and I creep into a largish village, stiff and with blisters. "This is a drab looking place," "Drab?" Francis snaps at me. "Do you know the hearts of these people?" There on a side street, is a boy lying on the ground, being kicked senseless by three others. Francis walks towards them, despite being warned not to get involved. He isn't threatened. Falling on to his knees, he weeps. The three boys laugh, but gradually, they become embarrassed, silenced by this little man kneeling in the middle of their street. People come out to watch. "I beg you to stop," Francis persists and the kicking stops. Drawing Francis to his feet, I urge him, "Come on. We need some rest". I breathe with relief when we leave the street. Well, for me, Francis is making a fool of himself. But I look back at the spot where Francis knelt. Holy ground. Fear doesn't put Francis off.

Read the section: Matthew 8:5-13

REFLECTION

Christianity is for the outsider, the exiled, the afflicted, the desperate. The Centurion, although a Roman officer, knew he was an outsider to Jews. He was desperate! His servant was in pain. 'Just give the order, that's all'. Maybe he didn't want his embarrassment, his fear to be seen. If I'm desperate then my prayer is simple. Desperation deepens and shortens prayer! Where are you Christ? Among the desperate, the disenfranchised who refuse to give way to resentment or the disease of cynicism.

I would bring you to wholeness that My Truth be revealed in you. *Bold*

EXERCISE

If you are desperate you will beg as you've nothing to lose. Maybe you've a desperation now. Name it; place it before Christ. See Him right in front of you: his face, his eyes, his mouth. Beg. Christ knew how to! In prayer, no one is watching, judging or measuring your qualities. Then calm your body, your breathing, your mind and then allow the sentence to drop into your heart. You will, through your begging, have opened it up in a way that makes prayer deep.

- - -

32.

PILGRIMAGE

I'm desperate for a wash! Francis moans, "My feet smell!". "You're telling me?" We laugh. So I remind him about someone close to Jesus who said that he would not only have his feet washed but all of him. "Good idea". So Francis takes his clothes off and plunges into the river. Sheepishly, I do the same, slipping into the river and almost have a heart-attack from the chill. Whoops and shouts and laughter. Close by, a monkish looking pilgrim, thin and serious, appears from behind a wall and shouts: "I'm trying to say my prayers. So shut up!" Francis simply smiles and shouts even louder, "Come on. Get in and learn to pray from the heart." "Who do you think you are?", the monk shouts. Do I tell him? "Pompous ass!", says Francis under his breath.

Read the section: Matthew 8:14-27

REFLECTION

Jesus appears to be 'done to' rather than working to a schedule. He restores, recreates circumstances to their true nature: a disease, an inner disturbance and an outer distress, become means of service. 'Leave the dead to bury the dead', he says: It seems dismissive if not shocking for Jesus to give what sounds like an instruction to leave the dead to bury the dead. This wakens the disciples up to the necessity of single-hearted determination. Healing in the Gospel is to enable vocation to be lived, creating greater opportun-ities to be single-hearted in the service of God in others.

I would listen for Christ in each moment and serve Him in others.

EXERCISE

The Gospel narrative portrays the divine culture into which I'm being brought. Prayer then is a co-operation, a collaboration with the Spirit of God that is bringing me into that divine culture. There are three parts to this meditation. 1. In your listening to others, to the world around you – its beauty and its harshness – what points you towards God's love and desire for healing? 2. Acknowledge where it is hard if not impossible to listen for God. 3. Listen now to Christ in you. Use the sentence to still your mind and heart and just be there in your listening.

- - -

33.

PILGRIMAGE

We're passing through a village where there's a forlorn grey-black memorial to those who had been summarily massacred for their beliefs, at that location. Tears come to Francis' eyes as he imagines the atrocity suffered by a forgotten people. We're silent for the rest of the day. At supper, eating rather stale sausage and sour milk, Francis tells me what he's been thinking about. "Jesus went with them into their hell. After all, he has been there endless times. Maybe these good people, like the swine, were carrying our destructiveness for us", he replies. "I was journeying with Jesus as I prayed for them." What was his prayer for. "For?", he replies rather wearily. "Maybe, I mean 'with'. When you and I go through another village tomorrow, on our pilgrimage, we must be alive to the roots of destruction. The Gadarene swine, with Jesus, carry that destructiveness that is even in us, that we cannot bear to look at." "In you?", I ask disturbed by and puzzled. "Yes. In me!"

Read the section: Matthew 8:28-34

REFLECTION

The details of this healing are disturbing and may even seem offensive. The two men recognise Jesus and, in the mythology of the 1st century, he becomes for them the Messianic figure: the one at the end of time who commits the 'demons' to 'hell': that perennial metaphor for utter lostness, appearing before the time expected. The presence of swine indicates that this was perhaps a non-Jewish region. Ritual uncleanness in the symbolism of semitic religions created a strong desire for purity; remaining of huge significance to the people of the Middle East to this day. So there is a double alienation, Christ entering both with his presence. This story might also be baptismal; anticipating Christ's death and and the incomprehensible perplexity of resurrection. The swine charge down into the water and are lost.

Paradise lost. Jesus is, perhaps, the one who regains Paradise beyond our comprehension.

In the rejected and alienated, find Me and serve Me.

EXERCISE

Emptiness of belief and absence of God often afflict those who pray. And yet, the God of love is paradoxically present. There is no experience, no place, not even hell itself that he has not already been. Allow the detail of this Gospel narrative to become part of you, even to the point of allowing yourself 'to charge down into the sea' with the swine. Then using the sentence you can in the depths (literally!) of prayer come close in your imagination to those who are alienated; excluded for whatever reason from their home, any sense of community, let alone family.

- - -

CHAPTER NINE – MATTHEW 9

34.

THE PILGRIMAGE

I watch Francis get out of his sleeping bag in the middle of the night, stand by the door of our bunk house and look out on the darkness. He's whispering as if in conversation. I can make out questions that started with 'Why?' or 'How?'.... No wonder he's tired. His prayer is a questioning of God. By the fountain in the middle of the village, at the end of our day's walk, Francis is enjoying a tomato, that was, for a change, fresh. Slowly four folk from the village sit with us, intrigued to know who we are. Before long, Francis is asking them questions about themselves, what's important to them, what's difficult for them. By placing himself 'at their feet', he's, like Christ, reshaping authority. "And what's your question?" asked Francis. "My question?" He laughs and adds that this pilgrimage is, after all, about asking questions, for which there won't necessarily be any answers. "Beware of answers!", grunts Francis in my ear.

Read the section: Matthew 9:1-8

REFLECTION

Christ knew what was going on in the hearts of the 'scribes'. They wanted to be forgiven but because of their position, they felt only threat. Too much face would be lost. Christ sees the 'fault-line' through all of human personality. In this story a paralytic, who is in desperate straights, has little, if anything, to hide. The 'fault-line' is obvious because truth is obvious in the sick. Christ's authority to forgive and heal, comes from the diseased through the poverty of their circumstances, because Christ is that poverty. Those who are not aware have not the poverty to face their desire for forgiveness. Perhaps I don't allow Christ in. To ask you to forgive me, I have to give away so much power and what I call self-respect. To ask a question from my urgent need is to give away power.

I would have Your gifts of forgiveness and healing through Your Christ arising within me.

EXERCISE

Imagine yourself carried in front of Jesus. Who is carrying you? Which of your friends would do that for you? See them. Let them love you. Imagine Jesus meeting with you intimately; looking at you and wanting to meet you in your sense of loss and pain, which tells him something of the real you. There's a poverty in your circumstances, no matter how rich you may be in some of your circumstances. Jesus is not just near you, but within you as you use the freedom to imagine him. He's rising with your feelings and transforming them. With the sentence, give your prayer enough time for this to happen.

- - -

35.

THE PILGRIMAGE

Francis watches a couple at a table outside the inn, tucking into a fresh loaf of bread soaked in olive oil, sprinkled with salt and gulping into a local amber-coloured ale. My mouth's watering and my stomach's rumbling. The couple have been walking for some time just in front of us. Fellow pilgrims? So, yes, we order the same and sit down beside them. They don't speak any language we recognise. We smile and laugh a lot but what we say to each other is incomprehensible! Before long, three others join us. To our relief, we understand them. The noise levels are getting too much for the rather sour-faced ladies on the neighbouring table. "Pilgrims!", sneers the lady with a little smelly dog under the table. "Loud-mouthed wasters", she hisses. Overhearing this, Francis audibly adds: "Let's drink to that!" Every one laughs, including the lady with a mouth full of rotten teeth.

Read the section: Matthew 9:9-17

REFLECTION

A combination of rugged truth and a delight in freedom brings about a realisation of the presence of God in Christ. Now, Matthew is called to follow. He's no spiritual initiate. He's an untouchable because of what he does; he's loathed. The Pharisees, with that pervasive disease of religious perfectionism, sneer at the people Jesus eats with. Here again, Jesus knows he is eating with the despised and they know he is as well. He is one of them! Freedom. That's where healing begins. And the enjoyment of eating together – Truth, freedom, delight – the presence of Christ.

My Truth within you sets you free to love and serve.

EXERCISE

When Jacob slept in the open with his head on a rock, he mused about his dream about angels ascending and descending on stairs, 'Behold God was in this place and I knew it not.' Not just in dreams but in straight forward enjoyable experiences, you may be able to say the same. Eating together can create delight, humour, compassion, learning and relaxation. Go back to a time when you had a meal you enjoyed in a group and relive the experience. 'God was in this place, and I knew it not.' Eating with someone is putting yourself alongside that person and in a way being fed by them. So in your imagination, who do you know who's poor for whatever reason? Imagine you are cooking for them and eating with them. Use the sentence as you imagine. In its own small way, this is intercession. Who knows what you might do next!

- - -

36.

THE PILGRIMAGE

At a cross roads, we're uncertain where to find the exit from the road onto the pilgrims' route. On the other side of the road is a woman about 50, sitting on a stone, with her head in her hands. She's exhausted. She's been trying to hitch a lift on a cart for over five hours and has given up. We don't understand her dialect. Perhaps she's a Romany. Does it matter? I whisper to Francis that there's little we can do. His eyes flare at me. He sits beside her, gives her milk and some bread from his rucksack. Nothing's said. Francis closes his eyes. After half an hour, he gives her some soap and a clean towel as well as money. Oh! And then he kisses her. She doesn't smile but it's as if the kiss has given her momentary energy.

Read the section: Matthew 9:18-26

REFLECTION

The woman was bleeding, poor and with that social taboo that surround women like flies, and to a certain extent still does. But this woman is desperate! Jesus is the servant of the desperate. Those around him in this story are either irritated or embarrassed. When you're desperate, who cares about religious niceties let alone insulting misogyny? Political, religious or any other kind of rectitude matter little when one side of your stomach is touching the other. The truth is revealed: 'Her cover is blown'. What is our haemorrhage: anxiety, unresolved guilt, anger, exhaustion? What matters to us so much that humiliation would be a secondary issue, if not entirely irrelevant? Delight in the healing that comes from truth...

Be still and I will reveal My Truth and My Life within you.

EXERCISE

One of the joys of meditation is that it doesn't really matter what you feel like. Your cover is blown when you pray! Nobody is watching or listening. Imagine you are standing before a mirror with nothing on and imagine that you are with someone important. What do you say and do? If that doesn't make you laugh.....! Laughter in prayer is so releasing. You have nothing on before God anyway! Now place before God the truth of who you really are, inside. Tell God precisely what your 'bleeding' is.... Then, using the sentence – relax and let God work on you. The desperate also know how to laugh.

- - -

37.

THE PILGRIMAGE

I'm looking forward to the walk over the pass and the view from the top. Francis and I have said the Office of Morning Prayer and there's Francis staring at something on the side of the path. It's a broken green wine bottle. The early morning sun makes it glisten to the point of being uncomfortable to look at. "Why are you staring at the broken bottle?" Francis replies, "The broken and the spent life of Jesus". "But broken glass can be dangerous!" I limply add. "So is Jesus." "Dangerous?", I ask, offended at what seems initially a cheap remark. "I'm summoned to find Jesus in danger, as well as in suffering or delight". Francis lifts the bottle, puts it on a low stone wall and carefully breaks it into smaller pieces of glass with a little rock. Gingerly, he places the pieces in a little bag. "Jesus broken up even more - even more dangerous!"

Read the section: Matthew 9:27-34

REFLECTION

There's a well known catch-phrase which comes to us from St Ignatius of Loyola: 'Finding God in all things.' But I don't know how to start. I've a 'dumbness' that lacks the ability to articulate, understand and describe even to myself what I experience of God. Oh for the wit and wisdom of William Blake! 'To see the world in a grain of sand.' Here's another of Blake's Auguries. 'The Lust of the goat is the Bounty of God'. Wonderful! But I'm not Blake. So is God absent for me? The concentrated inner cry for 'mercy' may open a door of perception. And the friend who understands me in my dumbness may open my understanding to a dawning of Jesus present in my 'finding'.

I would have the insight to find You and the freedom to serve You.

EXERCISE

Look over the past 24 hours and try and remember the sights you have seen and the sounds you heard, no matter how ordinary or disturbing. As always with prayer, don't analyse these experiences; just notice. Don't ask yourself where God might have been in these. Clarity may come in its own time, but you can't force it or manipulate it. Just notice and be aware. That's spiritual enough for most people! Use the sentence and allow the experiences to deepen.

- - -

38.

THE PILGRIMAGE

We're sleeping and resting for a few days, with the occasional gawp at what's around us, for good measure. Francis' snoring is seismic! Thank God I'm partially deaf in my left ear, but I've thrown one of my boots at him, to no effect. Earlier, two pilgrims came into our bunk room, while we were having some breakfast. "There's a group of us outside. We've heard that you are a teacher of Jesus' way. Would you teach us?" "On one condition that once I have taught you, you get on with your pilgrimage." So Francis outside, sees about twenty pilgrims staring at him. "What do you want to know?" "How to follow Jesus!". "Would you carry our rucksacks to the next village?" asks Francis embarrassingly. So they carry them! When we got there, they ask Francis when he's going to give them some teaching. "I already have. Think, and remember. What you have just done? Then I'll teach you some more." But they leave for something to eat – muttering.

Read the section: Matthew 9:35-37

REFLECTION

Crowds can be dangerous. This one is lost. The temptation is to have a leader who will dominate and unify people into action. Too often that action in history has been to fulfil the ego of the leader and the illusory hunger for certainty that such despotism offers. Jesus doesn't produce dominant leaders but labourers, working among the people – with them – not over them. The Church was not born with a hierarchy but with the attitude of service. The word for servant in Greek disturbingly can also mean 'slave'. Christianity, as Simone Weil describes it, is a religion for slaves. Christ is the servanthood of God, transforming slavery into freedom. Authority, then, in the disciples is Christ's authority of service.

Dwell in My Truth and be My Wisdom and Compassion among others.

EXERCISE

Leadership is important, but the question must be: is it Christ-like? All who follow Jesus are called to exercise some form of leadership through service. But the dominating image is a distortion of the Christ-like image of sacrificial service, let alone slavery. So in your time of prayer, is there someone you know directly or in history who has exercised Christ-like leadership? Imagine that person asking you to be and do the same. Use the sentence to 'ease' your way into the call of that service.

- - -

CHAPTER TEN – MATTHEW 10

39.

THE PILGRIMAGE

Two irritating pilgrims have joined us. Spiritual name-droppers! "Do you know who this is? This is Francis!" I snap at them; the name not meaning anything to them. Francis puts his hand up to shut me up. Then, even more irritatingly, they start to quote scripture, not bothering to ask any questions of us. When they unpack in the refuge, Francis takes me aside. "Ask them about their fear". They smile with that tell-tale smile of fear. "Don't be afraid, friends", says Francis. "Facing your fears will bring you stillness and acceptance." The authority of Francis' directness shocks them. One of them asks me: "What's your name?" "At last!", I reply with my eyes raised. But then Francis asks me, "Yes, what IS your name?" with a huge grin across his face. That shuts me up!

Read the section: Matthew 10:1-4

THE REFLECTION

Three processes are experienced in the first verse of this passage. First, Jesus calls his disciples to him. I'm taken right into Jesus, so that I know him intimately and live his life. Second, he gives me authority, not power for my ego. The authority comes from the struggle to live the Christ-like life. Third, this authority brings acute awareness. I can discern where the destructive 'spirit' is, and because I'm living in Jesus, my love is direct and present! How do I live the Christ-like life? Know Jesus deeply in the Gospel by praying Jesus. And praying is, yes, in love with him.

Live the Christ-like life and so bring My Clarity and My Love to that which is destructive.

THE EXERCISE

The Gospel demand on you is to know the Gospel intimately. In so doing, you'll learn about Jesus. To know Jesus, you're called to match his living by the way you live. This demands the gift of faith from God, that comes through two practices – a life of praying with the Gospel so that Jesus 'enters' you deeply – then practicing that Christ-like life in the smallest detail of your life. Failure or success have no significance in this. Perhaps by now, you might be seeing that having someone to accompany you on your spiritual journey would be helpful.

- - -

40.

THE PILGRIMAGE

We're late for the Mass in this little village, just catching the end of the Gospel. Fortunately, Francis has already looked at the Gospel passage (from Matthew!). The priest's unshaven. Villagers in the front pew, when they're not coughing, whisper audibly. On the way out of the Church, no one speaks to us. Pilgrims, after all, are outsiders. "That's where we are supposed to be," remarks Francis. Holding his hands out with his palms facing upwards, he says, "The Kingdom of God is near." He smiles and with his empty hands open, adds "The Body of Christ... for the outsiders." "Amen," I add, bemused.

Read the section: Matthew 10:5-15

REFLECTION

Jesus tells the disciples about the heart of His Gospel: 'The Kingdom of Heaven is near'. The implications of this are that the Christian disciple enters into another's, or indeed others' suffering. That entering is Jesus entering, because the 'Kingdom being near' is Jesus intimately with the disciple. My life-style as a disciple must be simple, in order that I can be constantly available to be of Christ-like service. Only then do the words that I use about Jesus have any depth to them, because there's authenticity in the way I actually live the Christ-like life.

I would know the fulfilment of Your Life through Hope and Service.

EXERCISE

Jesus enters you and His 'chemistry' of service is born deeply in you. Healing and service are important, but they arise from the love of God within you that is then brought into the places of greatest need, including death itself. When preparing to enter prayer, avoid worrying about whether you believe enough, whether you have enough information about prayer and about the Bible etc. You don't and never will! What matters is your realisation that you are loved. You discover the depth of that realisation in how you love in service. The first part of the sentence: Jesus' life in you – the second part – your Christ-like service.

- - -

41.

THE PILGRIMAGE

In my bunk, At 3.00am I feel nauseous, other unspeakable things happening inside me and from me!

At about 6.00am, Francis shakes me and tells me that it's time to move on. "I'm shivering and sick." I stay put in my bunk. Later in the day, I get up feeling wobbly. I catch up with Francis who's sitting on a wall. All he says is, "I've got the bug too. You've passed it on to me". Be careful of the authority of the saints, I say to myself.

Read the section: Matthew 10:16-25

REFLECTION

Rejection is what must be expected when the Gospel takes me into following Jesus. There seem to be three characteristics that lie at the heart of the gospel: authority, simplicity and directness. All of these come from the Spirit of Jesus. There's no consideration of safety or security. Even if there is confidence to be had in Jesus, that doesn't necessarily suggest that I'm protected from the anxieties and destructiveness around me. The desire of the disciple is to have Jesus at the heart of everything that he or she does and is. No particular slant is put on the Gospel for the furtherance of an institution or even personality. In our culture, to follow Jesus remains costly and support for that following will be largely fragile, at best.

My Spirit comes to you to deepen your prayer and your life in Christ.

EXERCISE

The significance of the word 'authority' is in the presence of Jesus deep within you. Get in touch with that in your prayer at the start. Then remind yourself of the importance of simplicity in prayer. Ask. What is it you really desire? Ask as often as you want to! Nag God! Then take into your prayer someone or a group of people that you are called to pray for. Do the same… nag! Beg! Then after you have lived with the sentence in silence and stillness, when you come out of prayer, be direct and look for the presence of Christ around you before you do anything.

- - -

42.

THE PILGRIMAGE

Francis is behind me. I'm walking with four other pilgrims. He's trying out a song. (He makes songs and hymns up. To be honest, they're not up to much and I've told him so. To which he simply retorts: "Well, at least I have a go!" I'm holding forth to the four pilgrims on my experience of Francis and his teaching. "And what has his Christian teaching done for you?" I'm now a little less eloquent! Later, now on our own, Francis tries out his new song. He smiles, knowingly. "What are you smiling at?" I ask defensively. "Impressive stuff, you gave that lot earlier", he comments. "I think I managed to get to them". "No you didn't", Francis replies. "Your mask did!"

Read the section: Matthew 10:26-33

REFLECTION

I put on masks because I'm afraid of being being seen for what and who I really am. Everyone does. Masks get you through your day. The challenge is to know what they look like and when you use them. Then, you can simply make the masks fit a little better. Being made in the image of God, Christ sees through all that. All is revealed. Not just the reality of who I am but what lies behind everything happening around me. The Gospel is, as the great theologian Carl Barth described it, the great question mark that lies over all things. Fear is more often than not the reason for not facing who I really am. My fear won't go away because someone tells me that I'm loved, but it might help me to see the shape of my fear, what I put on to hide it and, more importantly, what I can be and do to live with my fear.

Let the silence and the stillness bring you knowledge of My Love for you.

EXERCISE

Use the sentence for a while. Then, before you, in your imagination, is a bowl with beautiful, clear and cool water. Jesus asks you to drink from it deeply. Then wash your face with the water. Feel the sensations in all their detail. Do not dry yourself. Let your skin dry naturally. You look at Jesus before you. He conveys to you that this is a symbol of the water of baptism in you revealing all the darkness and fear in you with love. The water cleanses you and evaporates. Your fear is exposed in love and raised as a prayer of offering to be healed. When you leave your prayer, go and wash your face, and have a glass of water!

- - -

43.

THE PILGRIMAGE

I'm so unfit, despite the weeks we've been walking. I'm reassured because Francis is puffing and panting! Two women join us, looking lean and agile. One of them asks me: "Who is that man ahead of you? Cheeky so-and-so: telling us to stop gossiping about someone at home who wasn't present to defend himself. What business is that of his?" They come alongside him and I can see them gesticulating and then listening to Francis.

Later, I ask Francis what he said to the women, "Simple. I just asked them why they were so afraid."

Read the section: Matthew 10:34-39

REFLECTION

There are two basic kinds of conflict: destructive and creative. The first arises from despair and fear and the second from the hope and desire to live life to the full. Religion is not about feeling better from difficult feelings, but about the costliness of love. This can produce responses of rejection and ridicule. The language is one of waking me up to where my priorities lie. The demand is that I follow Christ and it costs not less than everything.

Let your love of Me be more and more at the roots of your words and your actions. *3 oL (| .

EXERCISE

You will never be able to love God, let alone anyone else enough. Brother Leo asked Francis at what point he would recognise that he has loved enough. Francis replied that Leo would never love enough. That's why Christianity is not a project. Projects are laid out to be achieved and finalised. Spirituality is about intimate cooperation with the God of Love within. It's a process, a journey towards openness and a growing trust in loving others into freedom. This meditation begins with the sentence to fend off any misplaced sense of guilt about failure or delusions about success. Then ask yourself these questions: Is Jesus my priority? What is the cost of this? Am I really prepared to go down that path? What help do I need? And, in any case, do I want Jesus? Do not force answers, just let the questions be seeded in you.

- - -

CHAPTER ELEVEN – MATTHEW 11

44.

THE PILGRIMAGE

Two pilgrims are sitting beside me. One of them mentions that he had heard that I knew the 'art of prayer' as a way of being close to Jesus. Such comments are great for my ego! So I set off giving them the wealth of my experience! Francis spreads his right hand in front of me. His index finger pointed somewhere. He's so irritating sometimes! He reminds me of the painting of Matthias Grünewald [excuse the anachronism] referred to in the section Matthew 4:12-17, where John the Baptist looks up at Christ crucified and points away from himself. "Perhaps the greatest characteristic the saint has is to point away from him or herself to…. 'the other', but also acknowledges frequent failure to do so." To hear these words from Francis whom I already am beginning to regard as a saint, is bewildering. "Repentance and forgiveness are the fundamental chemistry of the saints' spiritual practice", adds Francis, hoping I catch the weight of what he's saying . I then remember the two pilgrims. Did I point away from myself?

Read the section: Matthew 11:1-15

REFLECTION

'He will prepare your way before you'. The quotation in this passage is from Isaiah. For Matthew, the key dynamic is 'pointing'. The Old Testament points beyond itself to the coming of 'Messiah': the messenger-servant. So John, as a type of Isaiah, points beyond himself to Messiah Jesus. However, it is important to observe that there are two parts to this essential pointing. The first is that the 'pointer' achieves the attention of those around him. Once that attention has been 'locked-on', as it were, he then points to Jesus.

With Your Simplicity and Wisdom within me, I would point to the Love of Christ. *Bob)*

EXERCISE

How attention is achieved by the 'pointer', depends on the individual skills and personality of the 'pointer' – the John-the-Baptist figure. This can be with words. It can be with actions of love; through stillness and prayer. The beautiful but bewildering quality of the gentle persons of prayer is that they attract attention not to the ego, but beyond themselves. This is why spirituality is essential. Entering into silence is to look at Jesus and be looked at by Jesus. If you know Jesus in this intimate way, then how you point others to him ceases to be a matter of conscious method. Strangely, it is given. It just happens. Trust it.

- - -

45.

THE PILGRIMAGE

Francis is looking at some flowers laid beside some old walking boots of a young pilgrim who had been ill for years and had been determined to make a pilgrimage before his death at this spot. Francis is weeping and speaks of the young person with love. I lamely suggest that we pray. "I am. What do you think tears are?" I find myself weeping too. Prayer. In the evening, we find a bed in the local baker's house. Francis is still weeping. The baker took Francis' hand. "You come too", he says to me. The three of us went into the village hall and there's some country dancing. The baker doesn't wait and drags Francis into the dancing. Francis winks at me. "Mourning and now the dancing.... prayer!" The movement of God.

Read the section: Matthew 11.16-19

REFLECTION

Dancing and mourning. Of all physical activities, these perhaps more than most, express the body's wide emotions. Letting the body move rhythmically in dancing is an abandonment to joy, even, if you're not only ungainly on the floor, but also a liability! Mourning is also an abandonment. It employs a letting go in loss and not pretending to be in control. Wisdom in Jesus involves allowing myself to be abandoned for, even on behalf of others.

Let My Wisdom be the foundation of your living and your actions.

EXERCISE

Imagine yourself free in dancing, whether in the beauty of ballet or in the sweaty glow of country dancing with the accompanying sounds of sheer joy. Then picture yourself crying with copious tears, even wailing, over a tragedy. Don't allow yourself to be judged or analysed, least of all by yourself. This is a human moment of freedom and rawness. On the basis of those feelings, enter the silence. Freedom and abandonment aid the ability of the one praying to be in the present moment.

- - -

46.

THE PILGRIMAGE

We come to a shop that had some bread left and a basket of over-ripe tomatoes! A queue forms. Francis barges right to the front, lifts two loaves, some tomatoes and leaves money, without so much as a 'thank you'. Shouts and scuffling break out. Francis takes my arm and we force our way through the angry crowd. "Keep walking", he says. We're followed by angry women and squabbling hungry children. We go back a few miles, to a village we've already passed through. Francis walks straight through an open door to a young woman with three children. When he comes out, he gives me a piece of bread and a tomato. "What's all this about?" acutely puzzled. "To feed the really hungry, you have some-times to step over the hungry". He adds one of those irritating quotes from the Gospels: 'Beware when men think well of you.'

Read the section: Matthew 11:2-24

REFLECTION

Sin is damage done to myself by myself. However, in loving myself, I'm much more open in my attitude to others. There's a distinction between being self-centred and self-absorbed. From the former, I can reach out from the reality of who I am with my desires and fears. With the latter, I've trapped myself inside my own pre-occupations. Sin comes from the latter; love from the former. Further, groups and communities often behave in self-absorbed ways. When they do, they begin to deteriorate. Communities that love themselves, on the other hand, take the risk of being open to others, including strangers, inviting life and adventure. To love myself, is to give myself with confidence and simplicity.

I would have the courage to face my sin and, in the Spirit, be transformed.

EXERCISE

Become aware of the ways in which you have closed down on others. Notice the effects of that on yourself. You'll find, strangely, a lack of love for yourself. Write them down as simple facts without being overly self-critical. Don't make plans and projects that only serve to increase feelings of guilt. Then move on to the communities of which you are part: neighbourhood, church, association, working environment, etc. Are there ways in which these have closed down on others, have indeed been unjust in what is being said or done? Let the awareness work and watch what happens even in small ways in these contexts. Use the sentence to emphasise that transformation arises from self-awareness and, indeed, self-centredness!

- - -

47.

THE PILGRIMAGE

I try to get out of Francis why he's so low. "I've been trying to respond to people's questions and need for strength and, frankly, I've had enough." My fantasy about his endurance begins to fade. I take him to an inn for something to eat and drink, but knowing his reputation for talking, I tuck him up in his sleeping bag and bring him some soup, some bread and two boiled eggs. I leave him and with food in front of me, a young man asks me, "Where's your friend Francis?" "Exhausted and asleep", I answer. "The gentle and the strong will always have a great deal asked of them", replies the stranger. I looked at him for a while, and wondered.

Read the section: Matthew 11:25-30

REFLECTION

Jesus' gentleness and humility led him into deep conflict with the authorities. Where these qualities are experienced, there's threat to the existing order. Gentleness and humility call into question those who idolise power and abuse it, not by forceful confrontation but by an attitude of watching and waiting. 'Mere children' are defenceless and at risk from the abuse of power. However, they have that paradoxical directness that the truly humble retain. What's challenging to the accepted power structures is that the gentle and humble are 'done to' – as was Jesus.

I would wait on Your Gift to perceive and follow Your Will.

EXERCISE

Picture someone you know or about whom you have read who is a gentle person. Put some detail into that quality that you admire. What were the outcomes of that quality? Look over your recent history and remind yourself of the times that you were gentle. Picture also the place and the circumstances. What were the outcomes? These were moments when you allowed yourself to be 'done to' rather than you taking control. They were, as it were, outside your schedule. Perhaps you too experienced the need for strength in those moments. Now use the sentence and focus on the qualities of gentleness that you desire.

- - -

CHAPTER TWELVE –
MATTHEW 12

48.

THE PILGRIMAGE

Near a farm, there's a dispute about the boundaries between two houses. Threats abound. Francis, without saying a word, looks the contestants in the face and ushers them to follow him. At the disputed fence, he lies down on the ground and closes his eyes."What are you doing?", said one farmer. "Stop wasting my time!' said the other. Francis opens one eye, "I'll lie here until you realise that this land belongs to neither of you". Hours pass. No one budged. Francis stands up, "Come with me on my pilgrimage and I'll teach you how to pray for and even love each other". They don't, of course. But when they both return home, in bed, they realise how stupid they are. The dispute's over. The neighbouring farmers meet the following day. There's no argument but they wonder who that stranger was.

Read the section: Matthew 12.1-8

REFLECTION

The dynamic that lies at the basis of most religions is the inspiring life of a prophet, a teacher or an event that galvanises people to cluster around that dynamic. Inevitably, an organisation crystallises around the dynamic, with a system developing to manage the dynamic. The difficulty comes when the management becomes so controlling that the institution loses touch with the dynamic. This passage illustrates that tendency clearly. Spirituality is about staying in touch with the dynamic, using institutions and systems where they are useful and flexible and allowing them to be changed radically when they are not.

In Your Wisdom and Truth, I would grow in awareness of Your Presence.

EXERCISE

The Gospel's sense of 'Love' is always in the direction of love of 'the other'. When love of 'the other' happens, there is an experience of the presence of the Jesus. So when silence and prayer are disciplined, then you are directed by the Love of God from your inner life to 'the other'. Christian meditation is about moving inwards in order to move outwards for 'the other'. What really matters is the longing that comes from your meditation. That is why it is important to meditate no matter what you may be feeling like. Concentrate on this sentence. Don't repeat the sentence until you are focused on every word. Then allow God to love others through your longing for God.

- - -

49.

THE PILGRIMAGE

Today it's pouring! So we're sitting under a tree. Two young people sit beside us, full of praise for Francis, who tells them that they must recollect their healing experience from the day before. Later Francis tells me that the two had been walking for days arguing and rebuffed each other the rest of the time. 'How did you get involved?' I ask rather resentfully. 'I don't know. They simply stopped, waited for me to catch up and asked if I could help. All I did was to listen to them, look at them and love them.' I'm so jealous of Francis' personality. I too want admiration on this pilgrimage and it's poisoning me. Well, a little!

Read the section: Matthew 12:9-14

REFLECTION

When someone experiences the presence of God, or is admired and wanted by others, I'm inclined to feel that appalling poison of jealousy. What can I then do to undermine that person and stifle freedom? Although I don't have this destructiveness all the time, the fact that I have it at all is enough. 'My withered hand'... will I have the courage to stretch it out before Jesus, exposing the dark decaying part of myself? The man in this healing story said nothing. Nothing need be said when I expose the weakest part of myself. He had little to lose. Losing face is what stops me.

Receive the gift of Faith and stretch out your life before My Healing Love.

EXERCISE

What do you feel to be 'withering' in you? Look at your hand and 'see' it there. What do you feel about it? It may not be something that cries out for physical healing. It may be a relationship, a memory, a fear, etc. Now stretch out your hand. Then with the other hand use the sentence deeply. Receive. Then put your hands gently together, lay them on your lap and let Christ come to you through your repetition of the sentence.

- - -

50.

THE PILGRIMAGE

We're in a little church for a local saint's festival. We overhear an argument between the priest and a visitor, who's objecting to what the priest said in his homily.

Like many arguments, someone's right and someone's wrong. I suggest to Francis that he help, but he simply kneels in prayer. The arguers notice the little man and fall silent themselves. Francis' seems to be having difficulty breathing. When I sit beside him, I realise he's in tears. The priest and his adversary come to help. Nothing was said, but they realise what's the cause of Francis' sadness which he had taken into prayer and silence.

Read the section: Matthew 12:15-21

REFLECTION

Christendom can seem distinctly noisy and even egotistically strident whereas Jesus makes few if any assumptions. History is full of Christendom as the centre of the abuse of religion for the sake of power. And yet, there is a strange paradox, the gentlest Christians have often been the strongest. The ones whom we have to strain to hear, have spoken most effectively. Jesus wanted to avoid too many assumptions being made about him, as his Father's Kingdom was not yet realised. This psychology is particularly difficult when celebrity is admired and yet is so ephemeral.

Come to me and I will give you the Spirit of Love, Truth and Service.

EXERCISE

The desire to have your ego fed becomes an addiction, particularly in religion, where some personalities want to have spiritual power and have it now. The other even more poisonous desire is to be jealous and destructive of those who have religious fame and influence. In stark contrast to that, the Kingdom of God has as its focus the 'otherness' of God. There are tastes of it now, but there's always a part of the 'kingdom-process' that is not yet realised. We can't even imagine its completion, except through myth and artistic imagination. So establish silence that in itself is a placing of the attention beyond the desire for satisfaction. By the service of others, I enter into the life of Christ the powerless one whose authority is of God. That service is strengthened in the hidden discipline of meditation.

- - -

51.

THE PILGRIMAGE

I sit down to rest, as I've just stumbled in a pot hole. Francis gives me a massage. Wonderful! Despite my sweaty, smelly feet! We pray with today's section of Matthew, Francis providing the sentence from the reading. "Is there, was there anyone, no matter how appalling their attitudes and behaviour, who has been utterly condemned". "Oh yes! If you are expecting me to consign someone to Hell irretrievably, then I must include myself." He laughs. "And there's you, of course!" Another laugh. "So at least," says Francis, "We'll both descend into hell together!"

Read the section: Matthew 12:22-32

REFLECTION

Does denying the Holy Spirit really mean that we will never be forgiven? The forgiveness of God is the Love of God. To deny the work of the Spirit, is in fact to deny the work of forgiveness and healing. More than that, it's a denial of life itself, placing me in a self-imposed exile from creation, because I put myself outside forgiveness. The sin against the Holy Spirit is not about whether I believe in God or not. Belief in God doesn't really tell you much about someone's heart. I have found myself intentionally setting out to destroy Love; a terrifying moment: a 'hellish' moment, when I realise the ability and even wish to be gratuitously destructive. The passage says '...in this life or the next'. Is all lost? No! God will cross even my being 'unforgiven' in any world to come, hell itself, the greatest, unutterable distance from God himself, out of love. There's an incomprehensible aspect to whatever we mean by eternity. Metaphors are the ways in which I describe what it means to accept love and what it means to destroy it. By responding to them in love now, I acknowledge eternity's breaking in here now. The metaphor of being 'unforgiven' has its uses.

That I may perceive the Spirit of Forgiveness and Healing within me.

EXERCISE

To acknowledge that healing and forgiveness is happening means that you will be accepting change, transformation within you. That can be uncomfortable and create deep apprehension. There's an inclination to avoid it, there being a prevailing desire to resist change. That is, in a way, a denial of the Spirit of God. But what kind of God do you believe in that would make you a complete outcast? Jesus, however, is the acceptance of God and will wait, beyond your death, for an acceptance of love in its fullness. Let the sentence lead you into the deep silence of this mystery, this beauty! Now is the time to be truly responsive.

- - -

52.

THE PILGRIMAGE

We're caught with this massive bore by a village well. He's standing in front of Francis telling him what he's been doing with his life and all the people he's put right and pouring venom on all those who haven't paid attention to his undoubted wisdom! Francis can read my face. Now, we're alone. "You're bored with that man, I can see. Don't you ever get bored with me? I do with you! Thank goodness he's gone." "I agree!" "Ah! But…. I'm glad he's gone because it saved you from pouring out your bile about him in the form of false politeness. Nothing more poisonous!" A Francis cackle.

Read the section: Matthew 12:33-37

REFLECTION

There's a chilling poem by William Blake:

A Poison Tree

I was angry with my friend;
I told my wrath, my wrath did end.
I was angry with my foe:
I told it not, my wrath did grow.

And I water'd it in fears,
Night & morning with my tears:
And I sunned it with smiles,
And with soft deceitful wiles.

And it grew both day and night.
Till it bore an apple bright.
And my foe beheld it shine,
And he knew that it was mine.

And into my garden stole,
When the night had veil'd the pole;
In the morning glad I see;
My foe outstretched beneath the tree.

Live this poem.

EXERCISE

Imagine that you're in front of someone about whom you have difficult and negative feelings. Jesus is close by you, letting you be. Don't be afraid to express them and even to write them down, even adding what you would like to happen! If you do write it down be careful to get rid of the paper afterwards! Whatever you do, don't do this exercise on a computer! Now imagine that you have a watering can and you put the content of what you've thought, imagined and maybe written into the can with some water. Imagine pouring the contents at the roots of your favourite tree, or on your garden. Watch the results. Facing the real feelings is facing the truth and also the un-judgemental face of Jesus.

- - -

53.

THE PILGRIMAGE

The rain has stopped, but we're soaked. We're high and looking over the dark grey sea, with a huge swell so visible, despite our position. Wonderful sight! "Go on! Take your clothes off! Jump in!", Francis says. "But what if someone comes along. What will they think?" "Do you want to dry your clothes or catch pneumonia?" "That reminds me, Francis. You're known as a holy man! If I do catch pneumonia, could you....?" "Stop right there!" he barks. On a muddy patch on the ground, with his stick, he draws a huge fish. Underneath he writes; "The Sign of Jonah". "What on earth's that?" I ask puzzled. He smiles. That's holiness.

Read the section: Matthew 12:38-42

THE REFLECTION

Insecurity can lead to the desire for 'signs': assurances, indications of survival, something outside myself that will rescue me from an anxiety that dogs me. My seduction and, indeed, addiction to affirmation. Although being affirmative is a fine human quality, no affirmation is finally satisfying. To live for it as such is an illusion! Three days in the belly of the whale, like Jonah, is all the sign Jesus gives. Swallowed, in total darkness; lost... In parallel to other religious cultures, the ego that hunts constantly for security must 'die' in order that the True Self can come to birth that is 'hid with Christ in God', as St Paul was keen to suggest. But it's not just dying that is significant, it is HOW I prepare for my dying, so that it might become a gift to others.

I would be attentive to the Spirit's reconciling and healing of Creation.

THE EXERCISE

'Dying to self' is a tired phrase. 'Dyings' in the plural, of which one is my physical death, is more descriptive and, indeed, inclusive. Not to be free enough in heart, for example, to die to the hungers of your ego, can add to the damage of your environment. 'It's my space over against yours.' So enter into silence that's a 'dying' and wait for a moment. Look over your behaviour recently. In what ways have you wanted to exercise the power of your ego over against others, no matter how subtly? Who do you know personally or in history that has genuinely 'died' to the power of the ego for others? What has their life really meant? And your dying, is it a contribution to the care and freedom of others and creation?

- - -

54.

THE PILGRIMAGE

Fighting has broken out in a neighbouring country, with refugees trying to get across the border. Francis is listening attentively to the person carrying the news. Frankly, I'm terrified and too ashamed to show it to any one, including Francis – perhaps even to myself! In a little church, I'm kneeling, trying to pray and all I can feel is the fear and my shame at being afraid. There it is again: fear of fear itself. But I do tell Francis. "Why shame?" he asks. "Your first thought, Francis, is for the refugees, the injured or killed. Mine's for myself. Will the fighting come to us – me? Will I be at risk? Panic! I'm worrying about myself, my survival." Francis simply asks me to name all my fears to him. I put my head against his shoulder and weep like a frightened six year old child. Perhaps, the shoulder of Jesus?

Read the section: Matthew 12:43-45

THE REFLECTION

Most people in our culture have difficulty with belief in external spiritual entities such as demons, angels etc. Therefore, it would be all too easy to overlook the vital spiritual significance of this passage. Artists frequently talk about 'muses' that inspire. On the other hand, Winston Churchill spoke of his 'black dog' that marked a deep depression and anxiety within him that seemed, for a while at any rate, to bury his inspiration and courage in a deep pit of depression. One way I can look at this passage is to see myself with internal 'sub-personalities' that I can allow to have too much control over me: internalised 'voices' of fear, power, deception etc. Protecting myself from the power of these is one of the tasks of spirituality.

That my inner life may be strengthened for the service of others.

THE EXERCISE

Sub-personalities, some using the language of myth, might be called 'demons', drawing on ancient mythology as an imaginative way of facing the disturbing nature of fear and anxiety within. One of the ways of protecting yourself from their power is to accept and even to have an affection for these demons and understand them, for example, the image of a 'little boy or girl' afraid that comes from an experience of childhood that still can control some of your responses. Or there's the image of a 'dark frightening and angry man or woman' who sees every mistake you make, and judges them. Affection for these can heal and even use the memory creatively. Practicing affection isn't about being overcome by these 'demons'. Affection is a powerful way of coming to know. [Hence the well-known dictum from the Gospels: 'Love your enemies'] If they aren't accepted they can grip you and dictate your responses in ways that you do not realise. Worse, they can become destructive in others lives. Use the sentence to strengthen your inner life and be free of the power of the forces that memories can release. Here again, you might find it helpful to have the skills of a good spiritual director.

- - -

55.

THE PILGRIMAGE

A troubled young man's been catching up with us. Francis is irritated. Before setting off this morning, this young man had asked whether he might join us permanently. "No!" Francis replies sharply. "But I want to learn more about the spiritual path of following the Gospel of Matthew from you. I need your strength to face the journey. In fact, I regard you as a friend. More than that, I want to be a follower like this friend of yours." The young man points at me without looking at me. "You'll be a follower of mine," Francis replies dismissively, "if you leave me alone, learn the Gospel of Matthew, enter deeply into prayer and follow Jesus by living the Christ-like life." The young man pulls off the path and looks away into the distance. Francis grabs my arm and we leave him. I'm cross with Francis! "Ah! But remember: dependence only on God. Certainly not in or on me!" "Should I also leave you then Francis?" I smiled. He smiled too. "Good question!"

Read the section: Matthew 12:45-50

THE REFLECTION

In early Christianity, it took a while to articulate the image of unity that seemed to have been promised in relationship to God. The prophetic nature of Christianity is that it challenges all exclusive behaviour, particularly relationship and religious behaviour. This is disturbing, if not disruptive, to any society. Christianity is not, however, about taking people away from friendships or family life into some group, as has been the case so often in Christian history. To be open to the possibility that following the way of Christ might be about being drawn away from some relationships to experience insecurity to discover a dependence on the Love of God. That being drawn away might be temporary or even permanent, as in vocations to the single-hearted life in a religious community. But even that is not necessarily permanent. Leading a distinct life in solitude for a short or long period is not about living separately, but paradoxically about living deeply in union with God. In God we are all already one – but we behave as if we are separate from each other.

Let your heart be one with all around you through union with Christ.

THE EXERCISE

To be detached from exclusive relationships demands huge courage and possibly rejection. However, love cannot be love if it includes possessing the one I love. Jesus did not shun his Mother and his brothers, although it seemed like it occasionally! He knew he was already one with them, even if they didn't experience it. That oneness he also has with you right now. Enjoy it in using this sentence. You may not feel any unity, see it, it taste etc. Meditation is about waiting and acceptance. Hold to the discipline of praying in the inner Unity of God. Who are you intimate with and how much do you want to possess that relationship? Pray for freedom from that desire to possess and your love will grow as your Unity in God grows in this life and beyond.

- - -

CHAPTER THIRTEEN – MATTHEW 13

56.

THE PILGRIMAGE

I'm having a drink with pilgrims whom I have come to like. One of them wonders critically what makes Francis so special, particularly as Francis has been singularly unhelpful over news of difficulties back at home. His advice seems to amount to nothing more than: "Wait!" Soon the other pilgrims join in the criticisms of Francis. I start to collude with them; so easy to do since Francis is not with us. That dreadful realisation afterwards that I've enjoyed destructive talk of someone I love. "O God, why?" Francis is sitting at a table by himself but just, it seems, within earshot! Later, I find myself speaking to Francis about the pilgrims attitudes. He smiles at me, seeing right into me; unmasking my self-deceit! So, crest-fallen, I ask how to avoid getting caught in the negative slip-stream of others and my own destructiveness. His answer? "Wait, and you'll sow the seed of love deep in the heart. Oh! and, of course, watch your tongue!" "How do I do that?" I ask nervously. "Shut up!"

Read the section: Matthew 13:1-17

THE REFLECTION

A parable in the Gospels, on the whole, has one particular point to make. An over-analytical approach to Jesus' parables such as this one, may be interesting, but gets in the way of listening to the heart of it. In the case of the Sower, the uncomfortable sense lingers that there's not very much I can do. The seed will be sown in me. So the challenge for me is to wait on its growth. However, I must remember that nature can't be forced. The power is in the waiting. The word humility, comes from the word 'humus' meaning 'earth', the ground. And those that love gardening know the significance of humility in the waiting. In the parable, the poor quality of the sowing of the other seeds purely demonstrates how little I'm in control. Waiting is the attitude of expectancy and service. I like to consider it as the basic attitude in any spiritual practice. The best way to serve someone is to wait on that person. Practicing patience is essential and Christ-like.

Be still and wait on my planting and growth within you.

THE EXERCISE

Here's an opportunity to allow all images to fall away from your mind. The seed is somehow in the mystery of God sown deep in you. The planting is the work of Christ deep within you. Let Him get on with His work.

Be as still as you can and trust the growing. Use the sentence rhythmically and in time with your breathing. This practice helps to ease your mind of wanting to control and to create images that simply get in the way. Listening is only listening if you don't put your own construction and limitations on what you hear.

- - -

57.

THE PILGRIMAGE

"You're always up before me. How early do you get up?", I ask Francis, trying not to sound too inquisitive. "Early enough to be with God before you come and natter at me!" Why am I making this pilgrimage with such a rude man? Anyway, this morning I cheat! 5.30am, and there he is sitting on a log outside this hostel with scraps of paper. His eyes closed, he has a stillness that's conveys a kind of suppleness, an ease. Aware that I'm watching him, he asks what I want. "What are those papers?" "Well, it's my copy of Matthew's Gospel. It's fallen to pieces!" "What are you doing with it?" "Before you peaked at me earlier this morning, I read a passage and then allowed a sentence to arise from the passage, taking me into the heart of silence and the Gospel. How many times have I told you that now? But look at it, the rain during our walking has broken up the binding".

Read the section: Matthew 13:18-23

THE REFLECTION

In Jesus' explanation of the parable of the sower, there may well be a process that reveals itself. And, yes, there's some detail in the explanation. Some scholars have raised doubts whether the explanation is not a later addition, given the use of Matthew's Gospel as a teaching tool. From the explanation, what I sense in Jesus is that he sees seed as exposed to destructive forces through lack of understanding, or with no rootedness, there's bound to be constriction. Fruitfulness comes from energy given to understanding the Word of God, allowing it, waiting on it, to be rooted deep within the heart and an accompanying lifestyle that is uncluttered; giving space for productiveness.

Be open to Me in your understanding. Discover Me in your heart. Work with Me in My Love.

THE EXERCISE

If you're committed to spiritual practice, you'll give time and energy to finding God in all around you and then reflecting on that finding. However, that reflection must be deepened by entering into the heart and allowing the 'seed' of God to be planted deeply. That process in turn reveals an important critique of your life. It must be simplified so that the seed can be nurtured. Someone who is skilled in Spiritual Direction can help you with this process to discern ways forward. In the meantime let the three sentences work (be sown and nurtured) in the depths of you.

- - -

58.

THE PILGRIMAGE

High on a hillside, we come across two women and a bored looking old man, sitting on rocks a little way off the path. He's being lectured by the women. Francis stops and looks at them. One of the women shouts at us to come and help. We both sit beside them and ask if they have any spare water, as we're thirsty. They're too upset to have paid any attention to our request. "This is my brother", the woman says. "He's not joining in our Pilgrim prayers any more. He's so negative about the pilgrimage that he's disturbing our experience. And he's not acknowledging the dark forces within him!" "If I was walking with you, I'd resist your pilgrimage as well!", Francis replies in a chilling tone. 'Ask yourselves what is within you that is bringing about his response."

Francis slowly gets up, trying to restrain his annoyance. The three of them look at Francis, astonished and offended. Silence reigned!

Read the section: Matthew 13:24-30

THE REFLECTION

The prophetic challenge of the Gospel is that the only enemy within me is the one I create. To root out the enemy's weapons (the tares, the weeds) is to leave the enemy intact within, but they're not the issue. The burning by fire is a powerful metaphor for the work of the Spirit within that purifies the Self, made in the image of God and consumes all that's false; that gets in the way. The term purgatorial fire, purification, is strong in ancient as well as in Christian mythology. Fire purifies and cleanses as well as scorches and burns; at one and the same time preparatory but also terrifying. Indeed, images of what will bring all things to completion in God is portrayed by images of purifying fire. The parable points to God working within us alongside that which is destructive, not avoiding it; allowing it to be transformed by love. Thus, the Love of God has strong imagery attached to it.

Let your awareness of My creativity grow within you.

THE EXERCISE

The knee-jerk reaction is to find that the negative elements in you are somebody else's fault. You have, in uncomfortable honesty, created your own enemies. Once you see your faults and flaws as your friends, they lose their power! The sentence is an important means of dropping down into the depths of your heart and becoming more and more aware of the creative image of Jesus working within you. [A taste of purificatory fire.] That process, if allowed to work and given time, of its own, reveals that which undermines your life in God. Let the negative elements within you rise to the surface gently. Take responsibility for your own enemies within. The energy that comes from your living the Christ-like life will transfigure them in the depths of you with the 'fire' of the Spirit.

- - -

59.

THE PILGRIMAGE

Outside a shop, a young man asks me about what was special about my companion, Francis. "How's his preaching so powerful?" I tell something of his story: his colourful, extravagant, troubled background and his rebelliousness; about his preaching and his holiness. All

I get is glazed eyes! Then I remember. So I tell the young man of a little girl who had lost both her legs in an accident. She was being carried by Francis; he asking me to carry his rucksack as he had a sore back; how I protested about my anxiety over my sick friend who was far away, and I asked Francis to pray and carry him in his heart. Carrying another's load. That's how Francis preaches: with his life.

Read the section: Matthew 13:31-35

REFLECTION

In a sense Jesus is a parable. He didn't just tell them he showed them because he is the parable of the Love of God. How do you speak of God the source of all being, who is fully human? The paradox is too heady to engage with, other than in parables and metaphors. So a tiny seed becoming a huge tree or a hidden little piece of leaven bringing about fermentation: indications of the paradox of God's being in Jesus. Christ who is born apparently unnoticed becomes a universal realisation of God's love.

I would know Your Wisdom in my heart as Your touch of Eternity.

EXERCISE

The heart is the place of hidden spiritual activity. Move inwards to the heart with simplicity. Inevitably, the inner spiritual life leaves a sense of failure. There's a sense in which failure is the way Christianity works! But it's transformed, transfigured failure. Samuel Beckett suggested that he tried and failed and eventually learnt to be better at failing! In spirituality, there are no measurements of failure or success, because it's what you are that you face in the depth: 'The truth that will set you free' [John 8:32]. When the microcosmic event of pregnancy begins, there's nothing a woman can do to speed the completion of the pregnancy, without endangering the process. In a sense that is what prayer is. Allow this sentence to help you to be simple and let God do the secret growing from what is being sown in you.

- - -

60.

THE PILGRIMAGE

On a bench at an inn, we're having a long and blissful drink. We sit outside and look across to the mountain range that we'll soon have to climb. The landlady hands Francis a packet of letters tied with string. All are marked 'Important'. Francis walks back inside the inn and simply says to the lady: "Send them on to my brothers' address when you can." "But aren't there important letters in the packet that need your attention right now?" "Maybe", replies Francis. "But the pilgrimage is my first priority," he adds rather pompously. "Who does he think he is?" The lady adds tetchily.

Read the section: Matthew 13:36-44

REFLECTION

The explanation of the parable of the field is rather like someone explaining a joke. The tension is lost. The parable is all in the telling, the company, the context. There maybe have been, however, a desire to convey to the readers of the Gospel important material for teaching purposes. It's also important to remember that the Gospel was written among early Christians who had experienced the indescribable mystery of Jesus' Resurrection. Everything in the Gospel, back to chapter 1 verse 1, has to be read through that perspective; the perspective of shared experienced about Jesus following his death. The Son of Man, a figure spoken of in the Hebrew Scriptures, developed in early Christianity, into the presence of this 'Risen Christ'. That presence offers a glimpse into the fulfilment that mystical theologians describe as Union with God.

I would know the mystery of Thy revealing Wisdom within me.

EXERCISE

By entering into the depths of meditation where Jesus is, there's the 'field' [a more attractive image than the 'context'] in which he works in the tiniest detail of your life. Nothing will remain unexposed by his loving presence. The inner life, which tradition has called 'the soul', becomes more and more transparent. The 'angels' are beautiful metaphors for those experiences where you 'receive messages'. If you're aware of them, your spiritual life intensifies your attentiveness in this life and to the mystery, or mysteries, of the life you still have to come, including that beyond death. The sentence, if used slowly, enables this process to be stimulated in the depth of you.

- - -

61.

THE PILGRIMAGE

A young woman's walking by herself. Francis' smiles at me as he notices that I'm not only enjoying the fine sandals she's wearing but also her fine ankles! So is he! "I want sandals like that", I suggest sheepishly. Perhaps Francis'll lend me some of his money to go and have sandals like that made in the next town. "What's wrong with the ones you have?" "The pilgrimage'll be more comfortable, with fewer blisters". "I tell you what! Why don't you go and learn to make sandals; pull out of the pilgrimage and then you'll eventually be surrounded by the sandals you love." "But I want them now for the pilgrimage." So Francis, catching up with the young woman, asks if he could buy her sandals. She looks at us dismissively. "I could stretch them for you", she mocks us and walks on smiling. At least, my mind's back on the pilgrimage now, after feeling not a little humiliated.

Read the section: Matthew 13:44-46

REFLECTION

In the two parables about the treasure hidden in a field and the pearl of great value, there is a hunger to expend everything in order to have a single desire met. If I come clean about what I really want, two things happen. One is that I discover I don't want it quite as much as I had thought. The second is that I am not really prepared to give all, in order to have my desire met. The desire for God is costly. Looking ahead to the crucifixion of Jesus, I realise that when he cried "I thirst", he's exclaiming on behalf of a deeply needy humanity. On the other hand, I may find it difficult to accept and indeed relish the God of Love who wants me? Christians have held dear the image of God who pays everything, including death, for His desire for me. I wonder whether my desires come anywhere near to that I would have my desire to realise Your Presence of Light with me strengthened.

EXERCISE

Begin by asking yourself what you really want? Are you prepared to give everything for it, or at least a great deal? Then allow yourself to feel the desires that so often get in the way of your being free. You may choose to have a conversation about this with someone you trust and respect. What is the image of God that you desire? Perhaps write it down; a poem or even a drawing perhaps; a symbol. Begin the exercise with the sentence so that your heart and mind are open. Take the sentence with you throughout the day and notice all the other desires that come into your consciousness.

- - -

62.

THE PILGRIMAGE

A young couple are showing signs, when we catch up with them, of being unhappy, even distressed. All Francis says to me is: "Pray for them". "What am I to pray about?" Francis replies, "You don't need to know. Just pray. Your prayer has nothing to do with information that'll help you to feel better." Later, I ask Francis why he's spending so long with them. "Well, after listening to their story, they appear to be calmer, and I've become fascinated with their experience. I'm learning a great deal." "So, weren't you with them for yourself and not for them!" "Of course", he replies. "Have you ever come across anyone who loves someone else without gaining from it themselves?" "But isn't it completely selfless love that we should be aiming to give? Wasn't that what you were trying to tell me earlier?" "What kind of love is that?" he asks. I'm beginning to lose count the number of times I've become irritated with Francis.

Read the section: Matthew 13:47-50

REFLECTION

As the great writers of Christian Mysticism seem to suggest, all things are gathered up into Union with God, as in the image of the dragnet. I find the language of condemnation of 'the useless' difficult. If my life has no creative quality to it, there's a feeling of 'uselessness'. But what about those who are unable to be anything other than 'useless'? Even one look of love, however, makes the word 'useless' of no meaning. As Mother Teresa of Calcutta put it in a television interview: "Touch something with love and it becomes infinite." The point of the parable is to awaken me to be of service in this moment. I've come up with a new parable: "Blessed accept their uselessness, for their lives, hidden and beautiful, will touch someone with love."

Be alert to serving others as the imprint of My Presence here and now.

EXERCISE

Myths can be means to enable you to come alive here and now. They come from the world of story where scientific and factual information cannot grasp the depth of experience. Another way of putting it is that they're strong images which, in effect, are dramatised reality. Being alive is heightened even more if you discover the Love of God in serving others. That is where God is because that is where Christ is. Meditation with the use of the sentence (that arises out of the dragnet story), deepens your awareness and sharpens your sensitivity to what is happening around you. But, from the pilgrimage experience with Francis above, is this not using others for your own benefit? Yes! Why not, if, as a consequence, they are loved?

- - -

63.

THE PILGRIMAGE

I'm bored! The comfortable, familiar and the secure, I've left behind. What's ahead is unknown. Francis is sitting on a low stone wall, throwing a stone up in the air with one hand and catching it with the other, laughing every time he drops it. "I've been waiting on you to catch up. And – while playing with this stone, I've come up with a prayer that might suit you." I thought to myself how irritating it is when someone suggests something that might suit me or, even worse, be good for me! "Well, then, you better say the prayer." Still playing with the stone, he prays: "Jesus, arise within me and give me the courage to let the past go. Help me, however, to honour the past and use it. Rise through me and draw me into this moment, and trust in what is unknown ahead of me. May I be a bringer of hope in a changing and transforming world, particularly where it seems there is little hope. Amen. "What was that about?" I ask Francis. "If you're to be the Love of God, which you're learning on this pilgrimage, then you're going to be transformed. Risk the costly adventure and, yes, stick with it." Why couldn't he just tell me rather than come out with some prayer?

Read the section: Matthew 13:51-52

THE REFLECTION

I'm asked the question whether I understand. Jesus, however, takes me deeper. Understanding here is about knowing: being in touch with the world of the Spirit, which in terms of the Gospel might be called the Kingdom of God. The 'storeroom' is the memory, the world of the unconscious as well as the conscious. Spirituality is the experience of the rising of the Spirit within me through the old. The 'old' is that which is familiar. The 'rising' comes through that 'oldness' to that which is new and transforming. The 'old' is not denied and rejected, but not held on to.

Let the depth of your memory be open to My Healing and My Creativity.

THE EXERCISE

Remind yourself that stillness is vital to body, mind and spirit. To help you be still, it's important to have a lightness of touch and not to strain. The clenched-teeth approach to the practice of stillness won't achieve anything but, perhaps, the breaking of your teeth! To enter into the springs of personality involves, instead, allowing stillness to create an openness. Use the sentence for about 15 minutes - let its rhythm still you. Your memory contains images and feelings of past experience. Let Jesus rise within you, lighting on the newness, the creative desire within to serve the Love of

God. When you have completed this meditation, reflect, in writing if it helps, on what your response might be.

- - -

64.

THE PILGRIMAGE

Two pilgrims are resting on the floor in the house we've come to, belonging to a quiet generous old man. They're playing with dice. The air's acrid with stale sweat, not to mention colourful language. Francis can't help giggling at the risqué jokes, which gives me permission to join in the fun. The two pilgrims have no intention of creating space for us to lie down. "We got here first. Go and find somewhere else to stay. There isn't room". "It's raining!" I retort, miffed. Francis simply moves their gear over a little to create space for us. They grab Francis and me and our gear and throw us out. Outside with the door slammed, Francis knocks. One of the men opens the door ready to punch Francis. "Have this", said Francis. He gives the angry man his apple! But it doesn't work, he wouldn't let us in, despite the fact that he took it. No rest tonight and one apple between the two of us. Thank you, Francis!

Read the section: Matthew 13:53-58

THE REFLECTION

Possession is again portrayed as an inhibition in this passage. Relatives and friends are often spoken of as if they were possessions: 'my son'... 'our cousin' etc. Although this can be affectionate, it can be disabling because I'm no longer simply a person in my own right. Christ is inhibited by me if I 'possess' him; as if he is my sole property, or of the Church, or of Christians. From His birth onwards Christ, if he is the possession of anyone, then he is so perhaps for refugees. And refugees, by definition have few if any possessions. My freedom is dependent on being 'let go, let be'. Your freedom is dependent on my letting you go, letting you be. The Christ-like life.

That you may bring My Freedom and My Light out of My Loving within you.

THE EXERCISE

Even when you have attained a disciplined spiritual life, it's hard to resist possessiveness: 'my prayer-life; my heart; my feelings...' Sometimes even 'my spiritual director'. And they aren't yours. And then, there's 'My Lord'. They're, in the best sense of the word, intimately in your life, maybe. The Spirit of Jesus, however, is gift within you, not to be seen as 'mine' or 'yours'. The image of 'belonging to God' is a paradoxical one. To belong to God is to be free, putting into question all belongings. Ask yourself who you own; what you own; or what or who you would like to own. Are there ways in which your ownership has inhibited love and freedom? Use the sentence to reset where belonging really lies.

- - -

CHAPTER FOURTEEN – MATTHEW 14

65.

THE PILGRIMAGE

For several days fellow pilgrims had heard that Francis was on the same part of the pilgrimage, so had either waited until he caught up with them, or had raced to catch up with him. Instead of rejoicing at those who wanted to learn from Francis or to be inspired by him, I'm jealous! So I hang back a few yards on my own and look down at the ground, feeling humiliated: the 'Poor me' look. In the evening, they stay as we eat a light supper sitting on a stone bench at the edge of the village. Yes, I make sure Francis can see I'm sitting on my own. The next day, Francis walks by himself. I still don't join him. On the third day, I walk on my own without anyone, longing to be released from my self-pity! Francis doesn't even bother to console me. I wake up then, just in time!

Read the section: Matthew 14:1-12

THE REFLECTION

Herod feels acute guilt at murdering John, who had challenged his misuse of power. The presence of Jesus exposes the darkness that lies at the depths of human consciousness, with the intention, not of condemning, but of healing. To complicate matters Herod is caught in the trap of sexual envy and bitterness. What is exposed in the human heart is deceit, not by judgement and condemnation but by love that has an edge to it. Transparency and authenticity. John the Baptist exposes corruption simply through his own personal authenticity and the transparency of how he lived.

Christ of compassion, rise with Your Healing Light through the darkness within me.

THE EXERCISE

Richard Strauss composed a disturbing opera on the story of John's beheading: 'Salome'. It centres around the sexual infatuation of Salome, Herodias' daughter, for John. If she cannot seduce him and own him, then she must destroy him. Extreme maybe, but it may help to expose similar and perhaps unowned vindictiveness that lies deep in the psyche. It's one thing to want what someone else has, but it becomes poisonous when you long to destroy what they have, as you yourself can't have it. Perhaps the former is envy, whereas the latter is jealousy. The former is diluted sulphuric acid, the latter is concentrated. Allow the sentence to be the means by which Christ gently exposes the unresolved bitternesses that often are pushed down out of fear.

- - -

66.

THE PILGRIMAGE

I've forgotten to buy some bread and some fruit. We pass a group of people meandering and joking. You can hear their laughter from a distance. Most of them recognise Francis. He's well known for being short, thin and slightly angular. His beard is an apology for one! The group summon us across, but they don't offer us some of their food. Francis tells them stories and jokes. He then looks plaintively at them. "Have you had anything to eat? You look famished. And come to think of it, so am I" "Well, thank you for nothing Francis", I whisper in his ear. "Have you forgotten about me?" Someone from the group adds, "We haven't got enough for all of us." "Well, with the little you have, let's have a Eucharist beside the path." A shy old man in the group is stared at. Before long about 12 people gather around. The shy and apprehensive old man, a priest, steps forward: "This is my body. This is my blood." There's a silence and an unspoken expectation. He sat down and with broken bread, the Body of Christ, the group share and there's just about enough.

Read the section: Matthew 14:13-20

REFLECTION

Jesus responds to hunger. His life was not a project with an aim and objectives to meet. He was available and was more done to than doing. He responds even when he is at the vital work of prayer. In the passage, he gives more than people need, meeting deep desires and more: 12 baskets left over with all the symbolism of the complete collection of the 'tribes' of Israel being fed by God to the full and more. No fearful boundaries and no tight-fisted restraint in the Kingdom of God. If Jesus did have a mission it was, by love, to question boundaries. No wonder he was, and still is, uncomfortable.

In the delight and generosity of God, I enter into the depths of you to feed your hunger and desire.

EXERCISE

It's surprising to realise that so much of the Gospel is about desire and abundance, when the poverty seems so emblematic of Christianity, where it's called paradox-ically a blessing. So enter into this prayer time imagining that you are at a dinner party or equivalent. Enjoy this prayer time by imagining every detail of the food, the wine and the company you would like to be in. Don't be mean! Use the sentence to deepen your imagination and enjoy each moment. And what in inner life you may develop, in which you can entertain others, which is another way of saying that you pray for them. Savour the moment!

- - -

67.

THE PILGRIMAGE

A pilgrim, walking beside us, has just received news that his walking companion's wife has died in an accident. He's frightened of telling him, holding on to the information for days. He spends a long time telling me about his fears. "How am I going to tell him?" I can feel myself getting irritated! "Just tell him, for goodness sake!" But he drops back not the least consoled by my attitude. Francis is ahead. So I catch up with him and ask him advice. Without a word, Francis drops back too to walk alongside the frightened pilgrim. "Will you tell him for me?" he asks Francis. The bereaved pilgrim catches up with us and Francis asks him what he's afraid of. "Not being told the truth, even if it hurts", was his answer. At that point, Francis looked at his friend, nods and we leave them to it.

Read the section: Matthew 14:22-33

REFLECTION

In the evening, Christ prays and it's in that prayer that His realisation is deepened of the scale of fear in humanity. He doesn't condemn it, he comes to meet it where it is. Drowning is a terrifying prospect. Rejection, being alienated, feels like being drowned and forgotten. Christ comes across the water as a baptismal symbol, to 'baptise' Peter in his terror. Jesus puts his hand out and 'lifts' Peter. In Baptism, we have the dying [drowning] and rising [lifting] of Christ's crucifixion and resurrection.

That in the depths of me You would transform my fears by Your Rising and Your Hope.

EXERCISE

When I'm afraid, I feel my breathing become shallow. It's like drowning. There's a chill through me, with that tension in the gut. Jesus doesn't dismiss the fear, he points to the reality of its power and my lack of ability or strength in relating to it. Let Christ enter into your fears. Yes, that's easier said than done. Fear can so often render you feeling unable to move into prayer, let alone being still and calm. Praying is not about receiving pain-killers or beta-blockers, helpful though they can be. It's about what Paul Tillich, the theologian called, 'The Courage to Be'. Perhaps the words 'what you are and what you're feeling' might be added. Acknowledge what the fears are as well as what what you're feeling. Let Christ look at them and be with them as he 'holds' you, even if you're feeling so restless that the last thing you want is to be held. Instead, you can 'have the courage to be'. Use the sentence to still your breathing and deepen your attention to Christ.

- - -

68.

THE PILGRIMAGE

Francis has complained all afternoon that he needs to rest. So, I tried to get him to stop for a while. "I don't need rest", he snapped at me, sulkily. "Walking with a priest earlier today, I became angry and resentful. He sneered at my attempts to remind him of his vocation to prayer and love. I was pompous and condemning in my tone. What I realised my behaviour, of course it was too late. The priest left me to walk anywhere but with me. Pre-occupied with my own wisdom, I was seeing in him that which was lacking in myself." I take Francis' right hand and he takes my left and I gently soothe the back of his hand. He reciprocated. After a while we laughed heartily. The touch and the laughter of for-giveness and healing.

Read the section: Matthew 14:34-36

REFLECTION

Prayer as begging has been mentioned before on this pilgrimage. When there's starvation, men, women and children beg. It feels demeaning to beg. But when I'm desperate, it doesn't matter if I feel humiliated. Christianity is the religion for the desperate. Desperation is much more common in humans that we care to admit. When I'm in need, I feel that acute desire to touch, to hold someone, or something. That's what teddy bears are about. Yes, they're important. Even those with no religious belief will be inquisitive and even feel the desire to touch something if it has a sacred history. When a young woman came away from having lit a candle by the relics of St James in northern Spain, she was quick to say that she didn't believe it. But her eyes said something different. In her heart, perhaps she was saying: 'Maybe this will help me. Please!' Many of us, similarly, are keen to touch the famous. These are basic instincts, perhaps, lying much deeper than what beliefs may or may not be held. Touching Christ is the recognition of his presence in reality around me. Christ in flesh and blood. Touch Him!

Feel My Presence in reality around you.

EXERCISE

With someone you know, love and trust, hold each other's hands and touch them gently. Massage them and observe carefully the experience. This too is intimacy in prayer. But you don't have to 'say; a prayer. The touch is enough, because it's about loving in the moment. Then by yourself in silence become aware of your desire to beg; really beg God to answer your prayer. Feel it. Don't let analysis and defensiveness cloud your desperation. Imagine yourself reaching out to 'touch' Christ and 'feel' his strength and love 'massaging' you, loving you.

- - -

CHAPTER FIFTEEN –
MATTHEW 15

69.

THE PILGRIMAGE

Francis and I are standing inside a huge cathedral, full of pilgrims gazing in the dark at a single candle burning. Francis lies down on the floor! I'm embarrassed and feel like disowning him. "Lie down and look up!", Francis smiles. "Come on! Don't worry about what others think!" So I do, bubbling with resentment, and feeling myself blush. "Imagine that we're looking up and we can see the whole of the unknown and known Saints filling this space." Francis jumps to his feet. "Remember, don't try too hard to get your Christianity right. You can't do it without them, or these!" "Who are these?", I ask. Outside the cathedral there are the usual beggars at the door. Francis sits down with them, tells jokes and gives them some bread. "These! Yes, the Church!" He laughs again. I'm beginning to wonder whether I've had enough of this little man.

Read the section: Matthew 15:1-9

REFLECTION

Although lightness of touch is important in the attitude to tradition, nevertheless it has two creative functions. One is to keep me in touch with the stream of consciousness and memory in the activities and thoughts of our history as God is found in them. In other words, it's finding God now as I look at or read history. The other function is to enable appropriate change to be made in the light of experience. When tradition is maintained for its own sake, it can so often be a means by which an organisation, for fear of losing respect and power, attempts to maintain control. History is littered with religious organisations becoming self-absorbed and so, they atrophy. The change that may be necessary, however, may need to be made which will lead to conflict and rejection.

I would discover You in the experience of our forebears and in Your continuing revelation.

EXERCISE

Have a conversation with someone you trust about that which makes you afraid. What habits do you hold on to out of fear? What affects do they have on others? In what ways do you feel free to be flexible with tradition for the service of others? In what ways is there movement in your experience away from 'The Body of Christ' to seeing your spiritual journey purely in personal terms? Now enter into the silence with the sentence that you may be in touch with the long tradition of contemplative prayer. Allow yourself to be challenged at depth, to be transformed so that you can help others to face change. From this exercise, you may waken up to a challenge from which you hadn't bargained! As the old cliché has it: be careful what you pray for!

- - -

70.

THE PILGRIMAGE

We've had three days walking finding nowhere to stay, sleep or rest. Francis is getting scratchy! After an hour and half, I walk back and there's Francis sitting by a log fire staring at the flames. "Do you want to walk on your own from now on?" I ask him sharply. "Why are you so angry with me?" Francis asks. "I want to be taken seriously as a teacher as well, you know." "If it wasn't for you, I'd not be able to pass on the Christian practice to other pilgrims. Your love and care for me is not in what you say but in what you are. But, if I am not supporting you, Francis, forgive me." "You're free to be on your own. You don't need me." Tears. Why was I so full of self-pity? Francis is in tears too. I had wounded him and myself!

Read the section: Matthew 15:10-20

REFLECTION

A word that comes out of my mouth can bring beauty into being or it can set in motion cold or even hot rejection. In the context of social media on the internet, what I may write, even in a few words, can break relationships. The word that loves and creates comes from love, the word that dismisses or even destroys comes from fear. If I speak from love, then it may be beautiful or it may be tough, but not destructive. From fear, my words will wound or even alienate because of my desire to protect myself. When a group or nation behaves like this, the consequences can be dangerous.

I would have my words drawn from Your Loving in the heart of me.

EXERCISE

Perhaps when you are about to vent resentment in writing to someone or a group, just imagine yourself looking into the Face of Christ. Perhaps you might have a little reproduction of an icon of the Face of Christ, or have a selection on a lap top or phone. There's a caution here, because you'll have said or written something perhaps several times that have hurt someone. This is important. Don't dwell on what you may have said that has hurt others. Instead, recollect an event in which what you said may have delighted or released love in someone, no matter how small it may seem. As you enter meditation, picture the scene you were in and enjoy it. Then give thanks. This will help you move into your still centre, where you can use the sentence to strengthen the creativity of your words. Maybe the hurt will be dissipated by the indwelling of love in you.

- - -

71.

THE PILGRIMAGE

We're sitting down on the grass bank, drinking what's left of our water. Francis, after some silence, starts to teach me a simple way of praying. "It's called 'The Jesus Prayer', At least, my version of it." "Oh, come on Francis, do we have to do this just now?" He looked at me, smiled, and made no comment. He didn't have to. "First, allow your eyes to look around you and take in all you see. Breathe easily and calmly. Try to be still and don't fidget." That always irritates me. Francis sees my physical, not to mention mental agitation! "It goes: 'Jesus, God of Peace, have mercy on me'. Hold up your right hand. Say 'Jesus' on your thumb; 'God of Peace' on your index finger' 'Have mercy' on your middle finger, asking for love for all, 'on me' on your fourth finger, moving inwards to forgiving love for yourself, 'a sinner' on your little finger, acknowledging the distance you make between yourself and the practice of the Love of God. Then repeat the exercise until it becomes part of your inner rhythm." "For how long?" I ask plaintively. "For the rest of your life! But 20 minutes will do in the meantime! And if it's only 5 minutes, that'll do." He chuckled.

Read the section: Matthew 15:21-28

REFLECTION

'Lord... have pity on me!' By now, our experience of Matthew will have revealed a disturbing recurrence: how much the participants in the Gospel are desperate! The woman is a Canaanite and has at least two experiences of being rejected: gender and race, female and non-Jewish. The desperate don't even mind being humiliated or insulted. If I'm starving and naked I've nothing to lose. Is faith difficult for me because I've too much to lose? The 'cost of discipleship', as Dietrich Bonhoeffer put it, is truly considerable and without a deepening sense of the Presence of Jesus within, that sense will remain at best shallow.

Jesus, God of Peace, have mercy on me.

EXERCISE

The sentence is a Franciscan version of the The Jesus Prayer. The original form of the prayer comes from the Eastern Orthodox tradition, 'Lord, Jesus Christ, Son of the Living God, have mercy on me, a sinner', evolved gradually from desperate prayers that are recorded in the Gospels, including the woman's prayer in this passage. There are those who use little else in their praying. As you're on a pilgrimage with St Francis, perhaps you might try the version given in the sentence. The first half is adoration and the second half is the humility of beseeching, yes, begging. You can 'say' the first half with the in-breath and the second half with the out-breath. You can also feel the pulse on your wrist with the thumb of your other hand and say the prayer in rhythm with your heart beat. The prayer of the heart. In Orthodoxy, much more than in Western Christianity, when there's the cry for mercy for sin, the emphasis is on the Presence of the Glory, the Peace of God – Jesus, God of Peace. That's why liturgy should be as beautiful as possible: to give some expression to the inexpressible nature of God's glory, God's Peace. All Christian spirituality is in this prayer! You can take it with you everywhere.

- - -

72.

PILGRIMAGE

Kneeling on his bunk, Francis, with his eyes half open looks at the simple little wooden cross he always carries in his pocket along with Matthew. He lays it on the end of his bunk, on top of his copy of Matthew, with a look of simplicity, almost of naivety written across his face. He doesn't know I'm watching. He seems to have a love in him which reaches out beyond him. I have always, throughout this pilgrimage, assumed he has a special love for me. But somehow, I wonder whether that love is actually for me. After a while, he goes to wash, leaving his cross on the bed, with Matthew. I pick up the cross and turn it over. There, scratched on the back are the words as if spoken by Jesus himself: 'My Love for you is for your love for others.' That was a wake-up call.

Read the section: Matthew 15:29-31

REFLECTION

Jesus is by the shore; he is then on a mountain. Two images are striking here of Jesus being 'on the edge'. First, being by the shore, with those who were probably pushed to the edge by their circumstances. Second, moving up to where Jesus was sitting: relaxation and freedom to be open that being on a mountain brings.

The healings give a freedom to speak, a loosening from being confined, the ability to have the wider view, to walk and be expansive. So healing is not freedom 'from' but 'for', as love in Jesus is not love 'of' but love 'for'.

Come and be still with Me. Be healed by Me, so that you can be free for Me.

EXERCISE

Religious practice, in all honesty, can bring illness, hideous brutality between peoples, instead of bringing freedom and adventure. Religion can be terrifyingly coercive, in subtle and not so subtle ways. There's no getting away from it, but religion, Christianity [Christendom] can be the source of appalling hatred even to the point of genocide; the very opposite of freedom. Christian Spirituality is there to draw you into freedom: to be who you are, your true self. In the depths of your prayer, speak from your heart to God. Straighten your body out and be erect whatever your posture is. Have in front of you a painting or an icon and look with attention. Then stand up for a moment or two and walk slowly and carefully for a few steps. Focus on your movement. Adore this little experience of freedom, of God, that you have had. Then settle down with the sentence to deepen the experience.

- - -

73.

THE PILGRIMAGE

I'm hungry! Beside the road there's a rather run-down farm. So I knock on the door and ask if the old farmer has any spare bread and vegetables. He waves us in to share his table, which doesn't amount to much. When he puts soup in front of us, I can't help wondering about the contents! He holds his hands up for some silence. Francis frowns at me for looking so critical. The old man simply says: "God. Jesus. Spirit. These two pilgrims: gifts for the end of my days. Thank you." When we were lying down on dirty old blankets, Francis whispers to me. "There's a beautiful image in the Psalms: 'Can God spread a table in the wilderness? What's just happened?" [Psalm 78:19] Eucharisting, thanking.

Read the section: Matthew 15:32-39

REFLECTION

This story's possibly a retelling of the previous feeding story. However, it may be Matthew's intention to be insistent on the constant importance of feeding in Jesus' work: hospitality in inhospitable places. Again Jesus is available where convenience isn't considered, demanding a simplicity of life-style in order to be so available. There's a different take on the first story's blessing of the food. Here Jesus 'gives thanks'. Despite the adverse circumstances, Jesus' blessing is deepened by thanksgiving. I'm summoned to make sure that thanksgiving is a constant priority. That's the inspiration, of course, of the Eucharist: blessing, breaking, giving thanks and giving. These are the fundamentals for my following Christ that I may be in the presence of Christ.

I would find Your Presence in all things, and so give thanks.

EXERCISE

In the busiest time of your day, pray briefly and as intensely as you can that you may find God in the most crowded moment; in the detail of your day. Then, in your journal, whether literally on in your mind, note down what you experienced as a result of that intention. It's essential to have the habit of silent contemplative prayer that your spiritual antennae maybe awake to 'find God in all things' [St Ignatius of Loyola]. So enter into this sentence with expectation and imagine you're establishing the skill of a bird-watcher!

- - -

CHAPTER SIXTEEN – MATTHEW 16

74.

THE PILGRIMAGE

As we leave our lodgings, in the middle of the street, there's a brawl. Inevitably, a crowd's forming with shouting and screaming. Blood's pouring from broken noses, with the usual accompanying insults and threats. I'm appalled at the behaviour of the crowd, but to be honest, I'm secretly fascinated myself. "Violence exposes basic humanity, maybe because it's enjoyable!" Francis comments just about audibly and also annoyingly. Sweating with rage, I shout, to no avail, for the fight to stop. There on the other side is Francis, worming his way through the crowd into the clear space. He stands still with his eyes closed, despite being pushed and shoved to get him out of the way. The fight stops and the crowd stares at Francis in amazement at his calm presence. Prophecy by silence. We start walking, silently!

Read the section: Matthew 16:1-4

REFLECTION

To develop 'the eye of the heart' [St Paul's letter to Ephesians 1] is to have the insight of a prophet. Prophecy is the gift of seeing what is happening around me and finding God, no matter how life-giving or desolate the experience. This will lead me to have insight on behalf of others as well as myself that may be hopeful, sometimes disturbing and even at times decisive. Jonah was swallowed by a whale for three days, a powerful metaphor for desolate experience, and then spewed on to a beach: death and resurrection; both a desolate and a consoling experience. What seemed a curse was in fact a blessing. Desolation can be seen as, in truth, consolation and vice versa. Reviewing experience can lead to the insight that may differ from what my first response or reaction might have been!

In the reality around me, let me be know Your Truth and Your Wisdom.

EXERCISE

Discerning the presence of God in every circumstance may seem a tall order. It's not necessarily the same as being giving reassurance. Christian spirituality isn't about experiencing ease or even peace. That's not only cheap but, worse, illusory. Try taking into your prayer, with the sentence, an experience you've had recently: some event or exchange that you've observed. Ask that you may perceive the Spirit of God in it. Don't force the prayer. Wait and watch. Write down what you felt in your prayer and wait on clarity emerging.

- - -

75.

THE PILGRIMAGE

Francis is almost a day ahead of me; the first time I've been on my own for any significant period. My copy of Matthew is getting damp, like Francis' was a while ago, because of the constant rain in recent days. And it's pages are dog-eared and dirty! I do feel occasionally humiliated by Francis, even resenting the fact that he's my guide. All morning, I've been asking if anyone's seen the little man with thin face, wide eyes and a scraggy moth-eaten beard. One young woman tells me that Francis had said to her hours ago, "If a friend asks for me, tell him I've been here." What if he goes in one direction and I in another? I'm lost! I'm now in my bunk, exhausted and worried. But I remember him saying: "The wisdom of insecurity will guide you, which is the wisdom of Christ!"

Read the section: Matthew 16:6-12

REFLECTION

To assent to a religious system that claims certainty can lead to lending weight to the false authority to control someone else's life, including in extreme circumstances: rejection, persecution, leading even to crucifixion and genocide. 'That person, those people are denying my religion, therefore they are blasphemous, guilty of apostasy and must be alienated'. I can find myself colluding in such activity by my silence. Perhaps that's because I'm hungry for certainty. I'm deluded if I believe that certainty in religion will banish my deepest secret: fear. The dangerous 'leaven' of religion; all the more destructive, as this pilgrimage has shown, because the fear is not faced.

Through Your Wisdom, I would realise the freedom of insecurity.

EXERCISE

What's the gift you've received, the generosity you've experienced that has been given without any expectation, that has created a sense of freedom in you? Picture the giver and the gift. Go before Christ and hold it out to Him in deep thanks. Allow yourself to smile! What certainties have you been given? Any? Do you really want them? Generosity is an act that arises out of uncertainty, even insecurity, otherwise it wouldn't be generosity. Generosity is risky. Now enter your prayer and experience the freedom that spiritual insecurity, uncertainty brings. Here's the greatest praise of uncertainty: 'Blessed are the Poor in Spirit...'

- - -

76.

THE PILGRIMAGE

There's Francis leaning against a wall outside a prison. Tears are in his eyes as he watches prisoners arrive, pale faced, with defiance and fear. I'm transfixed by Francis' intense identification with them. With all the prison gates closed, I rush across to Francis. "I've found you at last," I say with a sigh of relief. "More importantly," Francis says in a low tone, "Find Christ. Or more accurately: be found by him". "Stop being so pious!", I retort angrily. "Where is this Christ anyway, other than in pages of this Gospel in our pockets?" Francis points to the prison and puts his finger up to his lips.

Read the section: Matthew 16:13-20

REFLECTION

The centre is the revelation of God. God becomes present now and that presence is experienced in Jesus Christ. Jesus is the realisation of God. David Jenkins, the theologian, pointed to God being as he is in Jesus. The terms 'prophet', 'Son of man', 'Christ' are of unfathomable but crucial significance for Jewish and Christian cultures. The disciples at this stage could not possibly take in this breath-taking encyclopaedia of theology. The silence that Jesus demands of me allows space for awe and understanding to grow within me. His insistence that their realisation be kept quiet is an acknowledgement that religious cultures, as has already been indicated, have the inclination to own, to possess creeds. Christ points beyond such imprisonment.

That in your heart and mind you may realise the Christ in you: the hope of glory.

EXERCISE

So the discipline, your practice of silence is the demand that you enter the Love of God in silence. The mystery of Love you'll meet in the silence of your prayer but also in small acts of Love, where Love can only be understood at a tangent and, because of your limited perception, never head on. Envisage where and who you think Christ may be for you: His Presence. Try writing or drawing what you experience in the silence.

- - -

77.

THE PILGRIMAGE

"Well. You have become very attached to me and I to you". Francis is giving me, showing me affection! About time too! And now, here it comes: the teaching: "You left me for a while and felt insecure. I've tried to teach you that there's a wisdom in insecurity, the wisdom of Christ Himself. You have learnt a great deal about prayer: the importance of daily discipline, of silence, of being formed by Christ through prayer and service. The conclusion of our pilgrimage is probably still a good distance away. Now you're ready to look at what it means to become more Christ-like." I laugh. "Me? Christ-like?" Francis' face darkens. "Of course. What do you think this pilgrimage is about?"

Read the section: Matthew 16:21-23

REFLECTION

Peter's attitudes were dealt with harshly. At one moment, he had been promised the powers of binding and loosing. In the next moment, Peter received another promise: the source of these powers would be killed. So the promise made to Peter seemed to him, futile. Futility is often the judgement I make when I'm frightened of losing control. The hard reality of Christianity is that the way to fulfilment in God for me is through suffering and death: loss of control. A denial of that can demonstrate how difficult it is for me to listen to God.

In obedience to the Way of Christ within me, I would be open to suffering with others.

EXERCISE

Following Christ is experienced in living alongside and identifying with those who suffer. Imagine in the silence, those who are or have been alongside you in your suffering no matter how insignificant: an experience of Christ being with you. Perhaps visit, write, email or telephone someone of whom you're aware is suffering. Get involved, perhaps, with a group that relates to those who suffer in some way. You're needed. You might spend 10 minutes imagining Christ's silent love alongside the suffering, with the service of your silent love and service. With the sentence, draw alongside that person, or group or people, and in the presence and Way of Christ love them. That is the power of binding and loosing.

- - -

78.

THE PILGRIMAGE

Francis seems to have eaten little for the last few days. He sits on a bench looking at the sunset. He asks me to join him, opening the palms of his hands and letting them face upwards. I imitate him. "What am I supposed to be doing?", I ask feeling self-conscious. "During this pilgrimage", he sighs, "I've come across so many people who're feeling lost and are hoping to find something, some way forward, some deeper part of themselves. Many are expecting an answer, and, frankly, I feel useless. So all I can do is first to open my hands and accept my uselessness as a kind of crucifixion; yes, me, picking up my own cross. Then I imagine I am carrying them. So, come on! Help me!"

Read the section: Matthew 16:24-28

REFLECTION

Notice carefully that Jesus indicates that the follower must take up his or her own cross. I've my own journey and my own response to circumstances. For the writer of the Gospel, some form of ending was near, figured in the Son of man's immanent appearance. This conveys deep within me the urgency of the Gospel. So, my behaviour here is not based on some moral code but an extravagant expenditure of life, a kind of 'going for broke'! Christ is with me in the sheer expense of his living.

Be awake to the expanse of My Love in you and from you.

EXERCISE

To enter into silent prayer is 'to take up your own cross'. It can include, perhaps, the painful discovery that nothing of any significance may lie at the heart of you, except perhaps an emptiness. Realising that prayer can deepen humility and suffering, is uncomfortable and bring suffering, as it deepens the centre. That centre is a place of strength and openness. Now, suffering here is about living in the heart of someone's pain or loss. For Christians, spirituality is not about righteousness or about self-development; some programme, some project, but it does involve an athlete's dedication, as Paul put it. It's looking out at the agony of a people and experiencing in prayer their agony, while staying; being steady with your powerlessness. Receive courage to use the sentence to enter this prayer.

- - -

CHAPTER SEVENTEEN – MATTHEW 17

79.

THE PILGRIMAGE

A young man in his early thirties, has his arms around the shoulders of a young couple carrying two tiny babies. They're exhausted. The young man tells Francis that the family had been ejected from their house in a nearby village and he's taking them to find some food and shelter. Now, the next village is at least 15 miles away. Francis says nothing, but helps the young man to create a shelter with branches. Although they are distraught, I can't help noticing that there's a distinct aura around the young man. "Well," says Francis a little later, "There always is around someone who acts out of love and compassion and around those who accept the simplest of help. You only have to look and then roll up your sleeves. Oh! I forgot to add: and allow yourself to be helped. Yes, you."

Read the section: Matthew 17:1-8

REFLECTION

Like all experiences of intimacy, what is actually happening in this passage is beyond analysis. Like all mysteries, what remains is to delight in it. The prime Hebrew Scriptures characters, Moses and Elijah with Jesus' dazzling appearance: all on a high mountain. Peter's shelters are like the tents in the desert lands that were set up to shelter the sacredness of the God-given Law, the presence of God. It's as if in this one bewildering passage, the whole of the biblical mystery of God's presence is recollected. The gospels were written in the light of the followers of Christ's experience of his resurrection. Maybe it's worth my while seeing this section as a Resurrection story. Jesus Christ is the present sacredness of God.

That your whole self may delight in My Presence going before all you are and do.

EXERCISE

Transfiguration is what you're about in the integration of your spiritual life, your inner life, with the living it out, your outer life. You might almost consider the word Transfiguration as the summing up of what the Christ-like life is about. The task is to bring God's transfiguring hope to places of darkness and despair. To enter into that mystery deep within you, imagine that you have climbed a mountain: one you know or one you imagine. Who is there with you to enjoy this moment? Your most intimate friends? Those whom you admire and have give you encouragement and example? Just let your imagination go! See Christ in front of you.

Even if it seems ridiculous, what would you like to do? Nothing much may come to you, if anything. Whether it does or not, use the sentence, simply to be here. It's good to be here.

- - -

80.

THE PILGRIMAGE

The early morning climb up the path to the ridge is a stiff one indeed! Francis is out of breath, it seems, but I soon realise he's moving his lips as if whispering prayers."Well, I'm just reciting what I remember of an Elijah story in the Book of Kings, particularly the one about being exiled in the desert and, after a storm and earthquake, finding God is the smallest breath of wind: the still, small voice of God." I'm amazed. "John the Baptist knew them and lived them," Francis says to me forcefully. "Knowing scripture by heart means what it says: the Word in the heart. Then you become the Word. Christ in you; yes even you! The Hope of Glory!" He smiles cheekily and slaps me gently on the back: "Christ knew scripture by heart. So he was able to use it prayerfully and passionately at the moments of rejection". Then Francis returns to his whispering. Prayer and learning by heart!

Read the section: Matthew 17:9-13

REFLECTION .

It's important to remember that in ancient times, human personality was not understood in such an indi-vidualised way as it is now. No one is entirely sure what are the actual words of Jesus in the Gospels. So, the words of Jesus represent his continuing presence in the lives of those who follow him. The Word is a personal experience, yes, but it's an experience held in the com-munity. Likewise, John the Baptist is the continuance of Elijah's uncomfortable warning about faithfulness to God rather than the idolatry of human power and acquisitiveness. John, who spoke of Jesus as one whose shoes he was unworthy to tie, is the prophetic warning of God. Jesus is the anointed suffering of God. Both of them are pointing to God's utter emptying of himself out of love.

I would be aware of Your Presence in those who point to Your Love.

EXERCISE

The central task of spirituality is that you are the Presence of God for the service of others and to draw attention to the causes of suffering among those who are alienated from love and human well-being. Silence, contemplation, reflection as a practice is the source of these two aspects of spirituality. So before you pray with this passage, it might be helpful to look at the story of Elijah in 1 Kings ~~and~~ again and remind yourself of the story of John the Baptist in earlier chapters of this Gospel. Take the atmospheres into your use of the sentence.

- - -

81.

THE PILGRIMAGE

We walk into a little house, at the invitation of a youngish man and there we see a woman, his Mother, sitting by a meagre fire looking distraught with anxiety. There on a couch is a boy of about 15 or 16, pale and thin, eyes staring straight ahead of him. "He's my brother," says the young man with terror in his face. "He's been like that for weeks." When I look at Francis' face, it's as if the same terror has overtaken him as well. He looks at me and whispers. "We must remain silent and imagine Christ's presence in the room. Work hard at your praying," he urges. "Prayer? Hard work?", I ask. "Of course." The young man is bemused by our conversation. "Well. Rather than just talk about it, are you going to do something?" "Leave us with him," is all Francis says. We're there for over 24 hours: no food, no sleep, but working with the terrified boy. The next morning, we return. The boy's sitting, with ashen features, but nevertheless alert. Is the boy healed? "Maybe. That's not the point," Francis replies. "Integration lies at the root of all wholeness. That's what Christ's unity within is about." I'm exhausted by the constant bewilderment of life with Francis.

Read the section: Matthew 17:14-20

REFLECTION

A sufferer from epilepsy can seem taken over by some external entity, not only to the anxious observer but the sufferer. In a culture where the God of history drove natural as well as historical events, such distress came from evil forces, 'the devil' or some negativity that is in the Divine. For some in our own time, this is still the case. What is important for me is that the story portrays the complete confidence in Jesus to extract the 'devil', because that's the nature of God's Kingdom, where restoration is free of destructive forces through the activity of love. I share in the disciples lacking in confidence in God. In Mark's Gospel, Jesus claims that the disciples had not prayed or fasted: a suggestion that the spiritual preparation I give to whatever I do is essential in the journey of faith.

In readiness for the tasks before me, I would ask for stillness and attention to Your Healing Wisdom.

BOLD

EXERCISE

Take out your diary or calendar. Let it lie on your lap or on the floor before you. Make it an offering to God. As you look at the details, having memorised the sentence above, gently repeat it after each item. If there is a particular task about which you are concerned, enter it in your imagination with Christ, using the sentence. Remain there repeating the sentence and being as still as possible. Breathe carefully and hold the diary with your palms open. Pray deeply that you may become more and more available for 'Kingdom' restoration work: working for local justice and integrity in whatever way you can, no matter how insignificant.

- - -

82.

THE PILGRIMAGE

At dusk, a small group of children with candles are enjoying the gentle warm light that they give out. Francis and I simply watch. One little boy says to his sister, 'My flame's higher than yours'. She blows her brother's candle out. He then, of course, blows hers out as well as the boy's on his other side, so angry at being treated like this. Soon, not only is everyone trying to blow everyone else's candle out, but they're throwing the candles at each other, causing screaming from the hot wax landing on skin, except for one little boy. With his candle out, he simply looks and remains still. He doesn't join in the candle throwing. Instead he collects the candles that are thrown away and lights them. He waits until all the children return and take, in silence, a relit candle each. Francis smiles. I've got tears in my eyes.

Read the section: Matthew 17:22,23

REFLECTION

For Jesus 'to be given into the power of men' arises from an attitude of deep self-knowledge and clarity. His attitude of non-resistance is one of almost assertive clarity. The power of his submission is greater than any oppressive power against him. If anything takes me into silence, this does. The story of Jesus execution and God's raising him is about the transfiguration of negative energies by non-resistance and the intention of understanding destructive forces that arise from fear. This dynamic approach through death strained the disciples' imagination and understanding, and still does!

I would enter into Your Divine self-awareness and so be an instrument of peace and creativity.

BdL Q

EXERCISE

The sadness, understandably, that you may feel when someone you love dies or leaves, can also expose feelings of possessiveness or dependence. In the silence, allow your imagination to feel the level of possessiveness or dependence in your relationships. Now, imagine you have this intimate relationship with Christ. Feel him telling you of his coming execution and 'sense' the absence of any suggestion of resistance. Use the sentence to deepen your understanding of the creative place of non-resistance in the practicalities and relationships of your life.

- - -

83.

THE PILGRIMAGE

Francis kicks my bunk. "Come get up, lazy!" "Why?" "Come and listen." So I grudgingly get up, yawning and grunting. Francis laughs. There by the fireside is an old man who has managed to walk the pilgrimage on crutches! Francis tells him that he and I'll carry him tomorrow. I drag Francis to one side and, through my teeth, ask why the man can't just wait and rest. After all he's got this far! "Because", glares Francis, "he's lived and prayed all his life with Matthew's Gospel. I've a great deal to learn from him, and so do you!" I snarl, "So we're carrying him for your learning, not his needs!" Francis smiles. "Of course!"

Read the section: Matthew 17:24-27

REFLECTION

There's no clear explanation of the story at the end of this passage. We're invited to enter the exchange and see the story as a kind of colouring of it, in all its mythic detail living now in us. But, there are themes. There's insult. Jesus and his disciples are regarded as foreigners, unwanted aliens, the disturbing nature of the ones that follow Christ with little if any compromise. Sensitivity to others. The collectors' jobs seems to be more significant than the new freedom of the disciples. The legend of a fish is probably an extrapolation from early Christian times when the symbol of the fish for a follower became common currency. The Greek letter 'X' became a simple symbol for 'Christ', as the letter 'chi' in Greek begins the word 'Christos'. The word 'ICHTHUS' in Greek means fish, the basic shape of which is like an 'X'. When the word was spelt out in full it symbolised 'Jesus Christ, God, Son, Saviour'. Perhaps the fact that it was a coin double the value that was expected rather than a half one, might be another symbol of the extravagant, even rash generosity of Christianity.

In all you responsibilities towards others let My wisdom be within you.

EXERCISE

Responsibility and freedom are dependent on one another. Let one test the other. A responsibility that is trapping you cannot be addressed creatively. Likewise what you may regard as freedom may be at another's expense. After you have been with the sentence in your prayer, play with the legend about the fish in your imagination. Expand it and make it your own. If you were in a dream about the fish, what would you find in its mouth and to whom would you give it? It's the kind of story Francis of Assisi would have loved and probably did! Playing with the Gospel may seem a strange suggestion. However, taking it as something that must be greeted with a constant frown of grim determined study, misses the playfulness of Christ. Indeed you'll miss out in the playing yourself.

- - -

CHAPTER EIGHTEEN – MATTHEW 18

84.

THE PILGRIMAGE

Francis and I have been joined by two students. One knew about astronomy and the other about trees and wild flowers. Francis nods politely at their knowledge. But they're not asking anything about our experience. I whisper, "Such arrogance". "No, no", Francis winks. "They're trying to find a way of asking me how to live and live well, but don't know how to. To ask me directly would be expecting too much humility of them." Francis turns to them. "How do I learn more about these magnificent trees?" After that, he lay on his back and asked the astronomer to explain what he was looking at in the early evening sky.

Read the section: Matthew 18:1-4

REFLECTION

All questions and comments, no matter how important or trivial, have their roots in a fundamental question: 'Do you love me?' It can be an embarrassing question except perhaps for children, lovers and those who are not anxious about revealing their insecurity. The further away I get from the basic question 'Do you love me?', to avoid embarrassment, the less honest I become and, even more, the less I'll get an answer. The child wants affirmation and knows instinctively that others response to the question is essential. The kingdom is where I can ask questions freely. David Jenkins described his own spiritual journey as constantly refining 'the question'. What is my question? Well, one starts this way: 'What must I do to prepare for death?' Then I must allow that question to be refined...

In the silence and stillness of your heart, come to Me in Freedom and Truth.

EXERCISE

If I ask you a question, I'm saying to you: 'You have knowledge about something that I don't know'. There's a saying on a poster that is attributed to Jesus but can't be found in the existing gospels, but may have come from the ancient church. 'Blessed is he who knows that he does not know. Cursed is he who does not know that he does not know'. When you do have the humility to ask, the question you put is not necessarily the actual question that you really want to ask. 'Do you accept me? Am I acceptable? Do you love me?' Yes, these do expose insecurity. Further, these questions can be asked in a manipulative way. They can be masked acts of aggression. Often in those circumstances, they are not really questions at all. The Kingdom of Heaven is where you can be straight forward and yourself. You can taste that Kingdom in the use of this sentence, following your silence with a few questions to Christ. What would they be?

- - -

85.

THE PILGRIMAGE

A young woman, gripped by anxiety, shouts for her three children. I can hear the children's laughter from a good distance away. Relief! There by the fruit stall is Francis. He's sitting on the ground telling stories and teaching the children to tie beautiful string knots. The young Mother rushes to grab her three little children, but stops herself, strangely entranced by Francis' gift with her children. "Untie this knot", Francis says to her with that cheeky smile of his. Afraid of seeming hard and foolish, she tries to untie the knot, but she can't. "Allow the knot to relax in the palm of your hand. Look at it and it will tell you how to do it." She at last smiles. She's a child too. And so is Francis!

Read the section: Matthew 18:5-10

REFLECTION

Drowned, hands chopped off and eyes torn out. The culture of the Gospels is one of urgency. And so Jesus' methods and style of delivery are often urgent and can be disturbing. The image of a child is one of total dependence: a model for relationship to God. So to relate to a child with kindness and sensitivity is to relate to God. The 'child' is not just an infant, but anyone who understands what it is to be utterly dependent. When I'm child-like I'm getting near to where God is. In our culture, such dependency is regarded as inadequacy. Indeed, dependency is seen by some as a pejorative word. The contrary is, of course, true. To depend utterly on God, whom we do not know, is what faith is.

I would learn simplicity from those who live in dependence on You.

EXERCISE

Abandonment or surrender is central. Go through your day's routine and engagements and hold them up against the light of surrender to God. If you think about it, you'll already have surrendered yourself to other people in one way or another and perhaps even to machines! As you use the sentence, imagine someone you know who has come close to this abandonment to God. What do you admire about him or her? Do you want to imitate that dynamic? Now take a simple activity for which you are preparing. Spend a few seconds holding it, surrendering it to God. Breathe deeply and gently. And let it go. Finish by praying for children you know.

- - -

86.

THE PILGRIMAGE

Between his feet, Francis is making marks in the dust on the path. "What are they for? Some game?" Francis smiles. "Close your eyes. I need your help." He gently and quietly speaks the names of people carefully. "Just have the names resonating in your heart as I say them and make some kind of mark representing them. Radiate love in Christ through the names!" I open my eyes and Francis is rubbing out all the marks. "Who were they?" "The people we have met on the pilgrimage, of course." "And you remembered all of them?" "Well, perhaps I got one or two of them wrong. But no matter, as I crossed out the marks on the dust, you prayed with your eyes closed. Thank you!" I frowned at the strange little man. He dug me in the ribs with his elbow. "Come on or we'll be late".

Read the section: Matthew 18:12-14

REFLECTION

If I lose something precious, its importance is in how it reflects on the image of myself. Losing something often means I've lost control of myself. So the rejoicing of the shepherd is about the interior relief and not so much about the sheep itself. That's not as self-absorbed as it might appear. The point is that the lost sheep has become very much part of the identity of the shepherd. If it wasn't, he possibly wouldn't care as much. This passage is about Jesus' identity, which is entirely wrapped up in others, particularly the vulnerable.

Let your personality be infused with My Life in your service of the vulnerable.

EXERCISE

When praying for those you know who are fragile for any reason, be aware of your own desire for them. This can so easily become a means of advancing your own needs, strengths and possessiveness. Not that your needs and strengths are unimportant. Lack of awareness of the desires around them, can get in the way. Imagine Christ to be with you, in whatever imagery or feelings help you. Use the sentence so that you can be 'with Him'. Christ's ownership of the vulnerable is paradoxically about freedom and release. In your local community, if Christ were to come, in the form of humanity now, where and to whom would you take him? Who is lost?

Following your answer to these, you may be opened to the reality that you are His coming!

- - -

87.

THE PILGRIMAGE

Achilles' tendon problems! Francis has been moaning for days. However, this morning, he's having an animated discussion, seemingly not noticing that the inn we're staying in has a stale and unpleasant smell. A group of teenage boys, wearing shabby clothes, have recently arrived in the village, speaking a strange language, to me sounding no more than a mumble. "With all the other smelly pilgrims around these foreigners are unwelcome", says the owner of the house. Francis staggers from the bench on which he's been lying, trying to rest his ankle. He's angry listening to the conversation of some of the pilgrims. "Let's chase these foreign louts out', a rough voice shouts. Francis shuffled across the room and joins the 'mumblers'. Anxiously, I whisper to Francis. "What're you doing?" "Mumbling", he replies. "Oh! And we're listening to each other!"

Read the section: Matthew 18:15-18

THE REFLECTION

There's a presence that lies behind what Jesus is saying. The wrong here implies harm done to the community. Personal ethics are important not for my development alone, but for the benefit of the community in which I'm set. Some ethical assumptions may need to be challenged and changed within the community. The emergence of the Kingdom may be about painful transformation but not about harming. The distinction is not always clear. Out of fear, I'm inclined not to challenge the 'closed system' of some community norms and that includes the Christian church! The 'Gospel' demand is that I'm to have the truthfulness and courage to challenge those within the community who have harmed, undermined its well-being by their self-absorbed activities, self-protective attitudes based on being right'.

May Your Wisdom and Truth lie at the heart of the communities of which I am a part.

THE EXERCISE

First, through a gentle review of yourself, become aware of someone who has had the courage to make you aware of your negative attitudes. Recollect the story, the feelings and the consequences. Only by that awareness can you, with detachment, have the gentleness and strength to approach others, concerning their attitudes, through listening and reflection with them. Imagine Jesus with you as you consider prayerfully circumstances of conflict which you may be experiencing currently. Be still and use the sentence constantly throughout this reflection.

- - -

88.

THE PILGRIMAGE

By the fountain in the middle of the village, we meet an anxious-looking woman in her fifties with a young man whom we've already met on the pilgrimage. Francis had asked them to join us for a while. The young man asks for silence, while the woman wants to know how prayer can possibly meet her needs. I want to give a clever answer but Francis puts his finger to his lips. "In prayer, I'm always physically restless," she admits. "Me too!", I add with a laugh. Francis simply says: "Listen to Christ in this young man, your walking companion." Then we're silent as each speaks, including me in my turn. A wonderful moment of gentleness, truth and simplicity! And what does Francis share? "I too have frequent moments of deep anxiety in praying." "What do you do?" The woman asks hopefully. "Nothing. I just accept that the anxiety is praying." I turn away thinking to myself: "Oh really, Francis." He notices. "Yes, really!"

Read the section: Matthew 18:19-22

THE REFLECTION

There's a key assumption behind Jesus' insight into the essential practice of prayer. If two or three people give time to reflecting on their common circumstances, confidence and perspective can be deepened in praying. Finding God's loving presence in all things opens up a little. It's out of this practice that forgiveness comes, not so much as a project but as natural response to the love given and received in the group. Because of the support and the inner depth gained by the sustenance that I experience with others in praying, the impossibility of forgiveness (70 times 7!) isn't the issue. So prayer and forgiveness can be the basic practices of small but open groups of Christians. Prayer is the essential resource; forgiveness is the outcome of the way we are in Christ.

That My Prayer within you may be deepened in friendship and practiced in reconciliation.

THE EXERCISE

This sentence is best used if you're able to be with a small group of those who meet to deepen their praying. It's important to limit the time for the group so that you focus on the task of praying. This kind of group work is not social gathering. Begin with silence and stillness and help each other with it by radiating your desire for deeper prayer for each other. Then listen carefully, without comment or debate, to the concerns of each person in the group for themselves and others. It's vitally important not to discuss the circumstances of someone not in the group. Remember the direction of the group is towards the work of reconciliation. Then enter the silence again with depth and expectation.

- - -

89.

THE PILGRIMAGE

"You look angry, Francis. Are you angry with me? You once told me that anger is fear expressed in a particular way." "Well, yes. I've heard you speaking disparagingly about how fed up you are with me sometimes." "So you're afraid of my moaning?" "Well, yes I am. But moaning is a kind of fear as well, because when you moan you don't want anything to change. You just indulge in your griping." Silence prevails while a recognition and a strange courage between us grows. Francis smiles again and I chuckle. Two over-sensitive pilgrims having achieved a new depth of honesty together.

Read the section: Matthew 18:23-35

THE REFLECTION

The early Christian communities had a sense of urgency. Time was short because political circumstances and God's perceived role in history suggested a drawing together (a 'judgement') of all things. The Kingdom of God breaking in demanded an ethical life according to the standards of Christ based on a truly awake spirituality. This parable demonstrates to me that the attitude of forgiveness is fundamental, because that's who God is. For my not to forgive, or not allow myself to be forgiven, no matter how difficult the context, is to deny God. The simplest and most difficult task in living the Christ-like life is forgiveness.

Be awake to My Healing Forgiveness within you and practice that gift among others.

THE EXERCISE

Be attentive to one person in your imagination about whom you feel resentful. That person perhaps owes you something; perhaps an apology, in your view, for the way you have been treated. Allow these feelings to come to the fore in you. Be there with her or him in the presence of Christ as you use this sentence. Then after the silence, address this question: what can I do to show that I'm determined to restore the relationship? Don't appease, but keep the possibility of communication open. It may be there is nothing you can do. After all, it may even be that reconciliation won't be achieved this side of death for the simple reasons that it can't be forced. Allowing the stillness of meditation to heal your resentment, nevertheless, is a vitally important start.

- - -

CHAPTER NINETEEN –
MATTHEW 19

90.

THE PILGRIMAGE

A couple in their fifties walk near us from time to time. But we don't engage in conversation. Sometimes they walk hand in hand and sometimes separately. They don't appear to converse much with each other. But this morning, Francis asks if they're related. "We're friends". They look at each other with a meaningful smile. "Love?", Francis sheepishly enquires. They smile again. "Our friendship only exists through love", the man replies. "And how do you love like that?", I ask. "Practicing, I suppose", the woman adds. "Practicing what?" Francis asks. "The hard work of loving in each moment, including this one." They both laugh. Francis' laugh is slightly strained.

Read the section: Matthew 19:1-9

THE REFLECTION

The journey to Jerusalem leads to Jesus' death, but that death for the early Christian Church was the 'day', with a sense of immediacy about the end of all things and the beginning of the new. So not surprisingly, there's an uncompromising tone to this passage. Sometimes when someone knows that death is near, there can be a sorting out of living, including relationships. Moments mori. Matthew not only points towards Jesus' death, but the necessary death of all things as a preparation for the Kingdom. So with Matthew under my arm, I'm summoned to waken up and sort out difficult and negative relationships. All my relationships, no matter how insignificant, have an affect on me and others. And that work is urgent.

Let me realise Your Love in my service of those You have given me.

THE EXERCISE

The word 'adultery' has a heavy feeling of condemnation about it, but that's not the point. Truth and simplicity are the marks of a lifestyle that's geared towards the Kingdom of God. There's an important aspect of Christianity about having a bag packed and ready. But this exercise isn't about guilt. The sentence draws your heart and mind to creative and loving service practiced in truth. What relationships help you to enter something of that dynamic? What relationships are in danger of distracting you from it. In marriage or friendship, in what ways do you compromise truth and commitment within it? It may, after all, be less destructive for you to disengage from a relationship than attempting to stick with it. Remind yourself that

Christ's presence recognises and even rejoices in the admission of brokenness.

- - -

91.

THE PILGRIMAGE

Sitting beside the path, a quiet and serious-looking man's playing a mandolin. What strikes me is how he prepares: sitting on the stone wall as still and yet as supple as he could before playing. When he pauses in his playing, he doesn't look up for appreciation or admiration, but allows the silence to carry the music through and beyond himself. Five or six of us are spell-bound; in stillness and silence ourselves. Francis approaches me and whispers in my ear: "Silent music."

Read the section: Matthew 19:10-12

THE REFLECTION

Being dependent on the Grace of God is not about heroism. For me to live in faith, is not about being heroic. And I'm relieved about that! It is, as these pages have tried to show, about obedience and trust. Marriage that's dedicated to loyalty can be heroic, but when it's a sign of the relationship between God and humanity, it's a gift of faith. Jesus sees celibacy as one attitude of single-heartedness: an active sign among many, a sacrament of the coming Kingdom; availability for sacrificial service. That disciplined single-heartedness is not so much an attitude towards God, but more from God to others, including those we love. Our love of anyone can be single-hearted through the gift of Grace. Celibacy, single-heartedness, however it's expressed, is not about denial, but about vocation. The days of seeing celibacy as among the highest of vocations thankfully are gone. Hierarchies of vocation in Christianity mistakes heroism for faith. At the very least, the practice of humility might teach me that.

Let My Light and Truth dwell in your heart and in your actions.

THE EXERCISE

Single-heartedness comes from a disciplined practice of meditation and, of course, life-style choices. The simpler the time of meditation, the better. Always begin with physical stillness and noticing your breathing. Refresh your memory of meditative practice from your own study, experience or indeed seek guidance from a teacher, a spiritual director. By an increased disciplined approach to single-heartedness in your meditation, then you don't need a project for your following of Christ. It will happen almost as a habit from the heart of you, which has been trained and gifted in meditation.

- - -

92.

THE PILGRIMAGE

In a remote clearing in a wood, by a little chapel, an old priest shouts at children chasing hens. Francis stops to watch; crouching down and organising stones on the ground. The children come across to watch. "Don't just watch!", snaps Francis. "Go and get some more stones and not too small." Before long, there's a huge mound. Gradually, we see there on the ground Francis is outlining a huge bird. The priest mutters, but the children try to guess what kind of bird it represents. Francis invites the children to complete what turns out to be a dove. One child asks, "Is that what you wanted?" "What I wanted?" As dusk fell, Francis beckons the priest to come over. "I hope you watched all this. That's how worship happens. Good liturgy!" The priest turns and walks away, grunting.

Read the section: Matthew 19:13-15

THE REFLECTION

So often, when I feel I have an acquaintance, even a friendship with someone who's admired or important, I want to protect my relationship with that sad desire to keep others out of the relationship. In contrast, to bring someone to Jesus is a common activity in the Gospels. But here, the disciples behave almost like personal assistants, even bodyguards; protecting their 'VIP' Jesus' time and space. Jesus, however, wants to allow the children unrestricted access to him without the intrusion of protective adults and their needs. So he expects the disciples to let go and trust in the children themselves. By establishing trust with children and they with him, Jesus can see through adults' but also children's manipulative behaviour. Acceptance, if I practice it, can flower through the simplicity and openness of approach based on trust. They too are marks of the Kingdom that is dawning.

Let the simplicity of stillness and silence, open you to the touch of My Love.

THE EXERCISE

Enter into the silence in the attitude of gentle noticing: your physical sensations, thoughts and feelings. Notice them and let them go. Give a little time to be aware of your breathing: the in-breath for stillness and silence; the out-breath for letting go. Notice what's happening in the breathing. In a sense, you're being like a child. Allow yourself to be brought to Jesus and to be touched by Him. Who would you bring to Jesus? Imagine the process and that you're being asked by Jesus to leave alone with Him, whoever you've brought.

- - -

93.

THE PILGRIMAGE

I'm finding Francis occasionally arrogant. Perversely, I find that rather comforting. Yes, he's attentive to the way of God, but not always! But, I envy his inner clarity and his being centred on the Love of God. We've just arrived at our accommodation. Francis has gone straight to his bunk. "Please just leave me. I want to rest and be on my own." He peeps through the slightly ajar door, I having pretended to go downstairs for something to eat. "God, I wonder if I'm just playing at this. I'm talking as if I've knowledge of your love. So many ask for my advice, but I wonder if what I share with them is based on a sham." As I listen, envy of Francis leaves me and my feelings are replaced by awe at such severe, even relentless holiness.

Read the section: Matthew 19:16-22.

THE REFLECTION

One image of God that has always challenged but excited me is of God as Absolute Good. Greek philosophy, so influential in much of early Christianity, saw perfection and goodness as qualities of the soul that needed to be reached by spiritual endeavour and thought. Jesus uncomfortably disavows illusion, in that perfection and goodness are impossible, as the disciples themselves experienced. So Jesus engages with the man in a manner that will waken him up to the illusion and, indeed, the danger of human perfectibility. He, like me, is left with these questions: 'Do I find God at the heart of all aspects of my life?' 'What are the implications of this finding in how I use my resources?'

I would find Your Light and Your Wisdom at the heart of all things.

THE EXERCISE

When you try to articulate your Christian living, it's important to remember that there's the 'never-the-last-wordness' about anything experienced or said. Psychologically, there has been incalculable damage done by a Christendom that believes that it's possible achieve perfection in the Christ-like life. This attitude can have a hidden destructiveness to it, producing so often a condemnation of those who are not perfect. Worse still, there is the nauseous wringing of the hands, literally or metaphorically, as I share my humility about my imperfections. This is nothing other than a hunting for admiration. Because perfection is not only not possible, but doesn't exist, there's an inclination to develop an unhealthy image of the otherness of God that's separate from us. On the other hand, God in Christ is the utter intimacy of that Love with you. So, let the practice of silence free you from what you ought and ought not to believe as a Christian. Let yourself be drawn into stillness. Let the sentence bring you into a process of freedom, discovery and intimacy. Don't worry about perfection. Let the image of it fade like mist in a breeze. There's a possible outcome maybe that may occur to you. Whatever possessions you assume yourself to have, you may just waken up to the fact that they aren't yours anyway! Another illusion gone.

- - -

94.

THE PILGRIMAGE

Fasting. I'm trying to lower the amount I eat and drink; at least for a while, and it's strangely hard on a pilgrimage. Francis is outside sitting on the edge of a well, munching bread, local cheese and a huge mug of soup. I'm proud that I've got through until 4.00pm with water and an elderly apple. Francis speaks with his mouth full: mangled crumbs and cheese spraying! "What are you looking at me like that for?" I can just make out his meaning. "This is a fast day", I say with a determined expression. "Do you feel better?" he asks. Infuriating!

Read the section: Matthew 19:23-26

THE REFLECTION

Jesus begins by saying that it's hard for the rich to enter the Kingdom of God and concludes by suggesting that it's impossible. The initiative for entry into the Kingdom is God's. So the rich are not alone. A camel going through the eye of a needle, even if 'the eye of the needle' refers to a tiny gate in Jerusalem's walls, would seem to inhibit anyone including the disciples. There's the common assumption that if you try hard enough and get your spirituality 'right', then you're 'in'. Even extreme asceticism can become another rich possession: the lust for being right and being seen to be. How do I avoid turning spirituality into another project that succeeds or fails, as if it's a PhD offering all kinds of kudos and affirmation? So, what's getting in the way of my having a trusting attitude in God who draws me into his love?

Enter into My Light and My Life and grow in trust of my gift of freedom.

THE EXERCISE

Spirituality is simply you and God in all your experiences whatever they are and with whomever they are. Practicing silence and stillness can bring you an attentiveness. However, the perplexing truth is that the experience of God is there for the most unlikely people in the most unlikely set of circumstances. Any exclusive spirituality goes against the grain of the inclusiveness of God. Your task may be to expose such distortion of the Gospel. It's worthwhile checking out with someone skilled in spiritual direction and practices stillness and silence, how possessive you are about your spirituality! But, remember to beware of spiritual experts!

- - -

95.

THE PILGRIMAGE

Walking slowly, Francis asks, "Did you notice that man who came into the hostel with us last night, asking me questions all the time?" "He was so boring", I sneered, but I'm easily bored, to be honest. The man had asked Francis about the meaning of evil; whether believing is essential and other such tedious questions. Dismissively I add, "You didn't really answer him convincingly". "Because there aren't convincing answers. Anyway, his questions weren't his real question, which he felt he couldn't ask directly." I'm scratching my head.

Read the section: Matthew 19:27-30

THE REFLECTION

The question: 'What's in it for me?' is important. Perhaps Jesus wouldn't have had any disciples unless they felt that there was something 'in it' for them: wanting recognition in the face of their seeming anonymity; wanting power in the coming of the new kingdom. These questions are ones that are perhaps too hard to ask. 'Am I going to be affirmed?' or 'Do you love me?' Any organisation, including a Christian one, can't function effectively unless there's something 'in it' for those who participate. For me, as one of those participants, to claim otherwise, is at least marginally dishonest. The reality is that I don't have any utterly pure motivation. The Kingdom's marked by the gifts of affirmation and love. Jesus recognised the importance of that. Few followers stayed around at the crucifixion, as there was nothing in it for the disciples after all and a great deal to be lost!

That I may be still and receive Your Acceptance, Your Love and Your Hope.

EXERCISE

No matter how busy you may or may not be, look at your activities recently and be aware of the ways you've sought for affirmation no matter how indirectly, materially or emotionally. What do you feel about that seeking? Then take those circumstances into silence and imagine yourself once again seeking that 'reward'. Jesus doesn't condemn the seeking. Now turn to Jesus, and imagine you are wanting the same from Him, now. Notice what happens and use the sentence to deepen your desire.

- - -

CHAPTER TWENTY – MATTHEW 20

96.

THE PILGRIMAGE

Francis and I are sheltering in a broken down barn from a sudden downpour of rain and we're starving. Francis is shivering and I'm trying to warm him by rubbing his hands, his arms and his feet, despite the smell and dirt. Making for a small farm house, we knock on the door and without saying a word, an old man shows us into another barn in slightly better condition, where there's straw. He brings hot soup and bread. Never has any food tasted so wonderful. The old man remains silent and leaves us. It's now late afternoon and we're back on the path. A pilgrim running, catches up with us, who had received the old man's hospitality shortly after we had. He tells us that, when he left the barn, he found him dead, collapsed by his front door. "He was one of the hidden ones of the Kingdom, wouldn't you say, Francis?" All Francis said was, "Act out of Love now! The next moment may be too late."

Read the section: Matthew 20:1-16

THE REFLECTION

So what seems a logical hierarchy in heaven is turned on its head: the last are first. There's no suggestion, as far as I can see, that the Kingdom is egalitarian, but neither is it hierarchical. Indeed, much as I may want it, there's no political or moral application of this story whatever. My assumptions are being undermined. Deserving, exemplary lives aren't necessarily about God and the 'Kingdom'. I'm quite capable of using my high moral posturing or defensiveness, as subtle (and not so subtle) means of control. Jesus, who is the Son of God, we might have expected to be the centre of attention, as he would soon become 'king' on a donkey in a procession. But that all came to nothing. He became the last and the least within days. This, then, is a story that prepares us for the Passion.

Through the simplifying of my attention, I would become aware of Your Humility in those who are powerless.

THE EXERCISE

The Kingdom of God is an image that you may find difficult: a reaction against hierarchy, perhaps with images of power in monarchy. The Kingdom's not a place set in time somewhere other than here and now. Nor is it entirely here in this present moment. There's a 'not-yetness' about the Kingdom as well. However, there's a taste of the Kingdom in you and your experience that's drawing you towards some fulfilment. That fulfilment has little to do with achievement or control. It's beyond life and death. So in the silence, allow images of that 'Kingdom' to surface. Write them down or perhaps draw them. If the 'Kingdom' is about the 'least and the last', recall the least or the last you have encountered recently and their circumstances. Allow yourself to feel a deep thankfulness for them. Maybe you yourself have experienced being the least or the last. Using the sentence, imagine Christ addressing you as the least or the last. Notice what he says and what he does. Imagination it may be, but that'll be significant for your response.

- - -

97.

THE PILGRIMAGE

A nun glowers at me at the table in this rather austere convent. She notices that I've had more to eat and drink than is good for me! "So here you are, about to say your prayers with your strange friend. Your life-style, it seems to me, bears no comparison to what you and he say about your spirituality". Hurt and humiliated, I pace towards her with clenched teeth, only I'm pulled back by Francis. "I suppose," she adds with one of those acid smiles full of condemnation, "You're another one who says one thing and does another". Francis smiles at her, "Why don't you sit down and join us?" "Join you? I'll meditate in the silence of clean air! You're both letting Christ down", turning away with an exaggerated sweep of her habit. "You're right", Francis calls after her, "But you could come and pray with us and help us be stronger. We could do with your strength." I scowl at Francis. He's an infuriating man and she's an infuriating nun. Francis only smiles and shrugs his shoulders, as the nun disappears paying no attention.

Read the section: Matthew 20:17-23

THE REFLECTION

Denial of reality is a common experience, particularly when an event may affect me deeply. This third prophecy of Jesus' execution is matched by Peter's three denials a little later. There' s an inclination to see Jesus and His Kingdom of God as some 'place', some utopian landscape where the followers will realise power and fulfilling the desire for egotistical admiration, a disease that is never far below the surface, the desire for egotistical admiration. Religion can be a playground for the ego, and particularly if I seek for power under the mask of spiritual righteousness or false humility. However, a mother naturally has hopes for her son who has followed Jesus faithfully. But, following Christ, the Kingdom of God is more of a process, a 'Kingdoming'.

'Taking up your cross', in some form, is a prerequisite to understanding the nature of God's love which is evolving all the time. Following Jesus, remember, is a verb.

Wait on My Light and My Truth, and be awake to their development within you.

THE EXERCISE

I want recognition. I want to be noticed. Being aware of that desire awakens me to its power. Jesus is modelling this process by gently heightening the awareness of his forthcoming suffering, in which the disciples, all of them will share. Move back into a memory of an experience when you've felt most abandoned; indeed when you've suffered most. Acknowledge them; remember them in detail and imagine Jesus there in the stories. Picture what he does or says. Then remain with Him and not the memory in the silence using the sentence.

- - -

98.

THE PILGRIMAGE

Despite the heavy, threatening and grey-dark sky, a tall thin woman joins us. She's excited about getting to know about praying with the Life of Christ, as well as the responsibilities that that brings. An old man who had been sleeping rough rushes up to the woman and asks for some money, but she refuses. "Well, take me into the hostel and buy some bread and hot milk for me." "Look. Not now! I'm on a pilgrimage and must press on." Francis takes the old man into the hostel for bread and hot milk. By the time Francis and I finish listening to his life-story, it's the afternoon. I feel sad for the woman's 'not now'.

Read the section: Matthew 20:24-28

THE REFLECTION

This section seems to go 'against the grain'. Jesus is demanding the impossible, at least psychologically. My image of greatness is turned on their heads. All too often, I make the assumption that by being a servant, I'll at best be used, but mostly ignored. Despite the fact that most celebrities claim not to enjoy their greatness, the desire for celebrity is addictive. The success of the media and retailing is dependent an that desire. In a sense, Jesus is freeing me from addiction to what some might call status anxiety. True greatness begins by my being aware of the insatiable desire for significance and admiration; then I can begin to find that significance in others, which is where Christ is.

My Strength and My Life are discovered within you through service.

THE EXERCISE

Most discontent comes from fear. Fear, in turn, is based on lack of affirmation or being rejected or humiliated. The desire for being noticed and my activities that feed that desire is a universal set of conditions. Spend some time in meditation simply observing the discontent within. Feel it, but don't judge yourself or anyone else. For some, discontent will be more pronounced than for others: raising disturbing feelings and memories. Allow Christ's own self-knowledge and acceptance to enter into you deeply as you meditate with this sentence. As you leave the silence, be of some service to someone: a letter, a card, a phone call, an email, a visit. Pray for that person. If you can, do it now! Don't put it off.

- - -

99.

THE PILGRIMAGE

Two envious farmers are admiring a herd of cattle. They're commenting that the herd must produce good quality. Their own cattle are in poor condition, it seems. Francis, hearing them, asks: "You want these cattle, don't you?" "No, No, No!", replied one rather unconvincingly. "Well then, perhaps you wish that these cattle were in the same condition as yours". They get angry, not surprisingly. An ugly scene is brewing. "But we can't have them, can we?" One mutters under his breath, "Pompous ass!" "Yes, you can", replies Francis. "Go and learn how these cattle are reared and looked after. Then you'll have cattle like them. And stop moaning!" I'm trying to hide! "By the way," adds Francis. "These cattle aren't the possession of this farmer. Maybe what you really want is to be seen as superior farmers. In which case, the cattle are simply for your egos". Francis can be pompous.

Read the section: Matthew 20:29-34

THE REFLECTION

The crowd feels that Jesus is its property. 'My' Jesus, often spoken and sung as 'My Lord' and that relationship mustn't be interrupted by you, even when you're asking for help. I don't see you as part of 'my crowd'. Perhaps, inside this crowd, I may be crying for pity because I realise that I'm 'blind' as well. However, I don't want to articulate my real desire in front of this crowd of followers, in case I become an embarrassment, ridiculed and then excluded. Jesus insists that those in the crowd name exactly what they want and take responsibility for their desire. I persist in avoiding that because I've a self-image that I want to protect. To name what I want might make me an embarrassment, bring ridicule down on me and eventually rejection and even exclusion.

Open your heart and mind that you may trust Me with your desires.

THE EXERCISE

In English, it's not possible to have any clarity in meaning, unless words like 'mine', 'yours', 'ours' and 'theirs' are used. But Jesus, the Word, comes to challenge the assumptions of language, not least because he can't be owned. He's not the property of Christendom. Jesus comes to you to stimulate you to take responsibility for all that you are, including what you desire. Use the sentence for a good stretch of time and then express clearly and simply what it is that you desire. Notice your feelings as you name them. Be simple, direct and don't try to be too sensible! Then ask Jesus!

- - -

CHAPTER TWENTY ONE – MATTHEW 21

100.

THE PILGRIMAGE

Now, it's time to ask Francis about this last phase of our pilgrimage, but he simply remains very still and silent. However, I don't feel excluded from his silence. It's as if I'm invited into another pilgrimage; one that's running parallel to it. His silence lays palms down on the path, as it were, for me to process into the silence with him. So I sit and, believe it or not, I'm still. When we come out of the silence half an hour later, I ask a rather silly question. "Well what now?" "Say or sing 'Hosanna!' silently." Two pilgrimages, the outer and the inner, are one.

Read the section: Matthew 21:1-11

THE REFLECTION

Three images of insignificance are paradoxically striking. One is Jesus' procession on a donkey. The second is the contrast between the insignificant Nazareth and the religiously self-conscious Jerusalem. The third is the carpet of palm branches. But this is no cheap or shoddily prepared event, let alone some veiled satyr. The crowds suggest that these symbols are important. In retrospect, I notice the natural cross on a donkey's back. A week later, the 'Hosannas' would sound differently. When the going is easy I either find praising easy. When it's difficult, I forget, too pre-occupied with my own fears. Maybe my 'Hosannas' would sound hollow anyway. There's a danger that, because of my self-absorption, I miss in this story Jesus and his procession's prophetic challenging by symbols of religious power, the ecclesiastical authorities.

I would have my attitudes and actions transfigured by Your Humility and Strength.

THE EXERCISE

By establishing stillness, even if it's only for a few moments, you've experienced a little humility, because you've let at least some of perceptions and mispercep-tions of yourself go. Contemplative prayer happens when the hard work of facing the truth of who you really are has been practiced constantly. There are no obvious achievements and rewards. There's just you and God, and even God is imperceivable. The life of inner praying is an act of love and self-giving that takes the risk of emptiness. St Paul described Jesus' work in this way: he emptied himself, taking the form of a slave. Praying at this depth is devoid of power. There's a building up of hope, however. Spend time thinking of circumstances where power is exercised against the challenge of love. Then become aware of ways in which you perhaps collude with the engines of power. Perhaps there are ways in which you can model the way of humility and its strength. Don't force it. Allow the sentence to build up attention in you and the action to arise out of it will surface.

- - -

101.

THE PILGRIMAGE

Francis has an infected heel as a result of a huge blister, which he hadn't looked after properly. So we stand in a queue to see an old lady who can help. Three men are leaning across the counter and wagging their fingers at the old lady, telling her that she ought to sell their medicines, as hers are out-dated and useless. They're not aware that the old lady listens to people, almost, to them, as if her medicines, which she gives out freely, are beside the point. Francis nudges to the front of the queue, and shouts, "Out!" The old lady looks at Francis' heel. She shakes her head and looks at him. "I know, I know," Francis sighs.

Read the section: Matthew 21:12-17

THE REFLECTION

This act of assertiveness, if not aggression, challenges my perception of Jesus as emotionally controlled. Persuading people, no matter how surreptitiously, for the sale of goods or for their adherence misses the point and is a kind of high-jacking. Sacred places are for prayer and not for canvassing, persuasion or indeed proselytism for that matter. Proselytism is so often a mask for the execution of power based on fear. The one who prays comes in to a church in order to offer him or herself, not to become an object of marketing. Although sacred places must be attractive through the arts and architecture, they aren't centres for attracting custom. Sounds of children shouting aren't often encouraged in sacred places and I've frowned at intrusive sounds getting in my way. Jesus encourages them because they're the simple and direct offering of their lives.

Let the sacredness of place and of time be a focus of your pilgrimage into My Holiness.

THE EXERCISE

Sacred places are not always easy to find. Often they are beset with the need for survival both economically or architecturally, or both. They can so easily become centres of commerce. That, however, is also true of your inner life. In your imagination, invite Jesus to enter your life and kick over a few bits of 'furniture' or even 'people' [!] that clutter your inner life, its imagination and feelings. Perhaps Jesus might throw out the grasping desires that create distraction and even pain. Your heart, remember, is a sacred space. Use the sentence so that Christ can reclaim it for the holiness of your pilgrimage.

- - -

102.

THE PILGRIMAGE

Because of the cold and winds, Francis and I are finding it hard to keep going. At a place where paths cross, we had found it difficult to know which direction to take. We've come across an old evergreen tree, its wind-swept shape created by the prevailing winds. Francis gazes at the tree as if he's meditating, while I'm getting cold. "Come on Francis, let's keep moving, please!" But he doesn't move. Instead, he falls to his knees in prayer before the tree. "Can't you see?", he snaps, "We're being invited not simply to read about the Passion. This tree is speaking: 'Be the Passion!'"

Read the section: Matthew 21:18-22

THE REFLECTION

The word vandalism comes to my mind. However, I find understanding this story is difficult, given the period of history in which the gospel was probably written and the consequent difference in cultural assumptions. Authority over nature itself was regarded as a mark of divinity. Although allegorical interpretation isn't practiced as it once was, the fig tree that bears no fruit might be paralleled with the tree, the cross, that did bear the fruit of forgiveness, particularly as the story is placed just before the Passion. The heart of the story is faith and prayer. The starkness of the story illustrates the utter centrality of God in and over all things. I'm left with a question mark about the tree that is a metaphor for my life.

That in your stillness you may Receive My Gift of Faith and have My Grace to live it.

THE EXERCISE

In the Middle and Far Eastern religious cultures, the story of God is portrayed in myth. Myth is truth told 'at a tangent', because there isn't any other way of doing so. Unfortunately, myth, legend, allegory, parable, metaphor and fable are used almost synonymously. How do you understand the word myth? Perhaps do a little research. If you were invited to tell a group about faith and prayer, as you understand it, perhaps you would use story, a myth. The details of the story may not be factual, but at its heart, truth is conveyed. Perhaps you can think of stories that are myths and have conveyed deep truth for you. In the stillness begin with the sentence; tell a brief story that comes from you about the centrality of faith and prayer for you. Perhaps afterwards, you may want to write it down. Then with a friend or spiritual director tease out how you live out the faith given you.

- - -

103.

THE PILGRIMAGE

"What's on your mind today?", Francis asks, looking piercingly into my eyes. "I've just been trying to remember my Mother." "What was she like?" "Towards the end of her life, she was disturbed and even angry, about anything, particularly about me." Francis looks into the distance in silence and asks, "Would you help me with understanding and relating to my Mother?" Francis' questions are as much a revelation of his authority as of his humility. How much people reveal fears in themselves when they feel they have too much to lose to ask questions.

Read the section: Matthew 21:23-27

THE REFLECTION

Jesus frequently acts as teacher. I suspect I like the education I want or feel comfortable with. Education can
be much more than that: an increase in my understanding of myself and that's not necessarily what I
want! Jesus' authority was right in the heart of what
education is about. He recognised a hunger and so he
fed it. However, he also engaged with ambiguity, irony,
parable and metaphor as a means of including those
whom he reckoned largely didn't want to 'hear'. When
authority has become an issue between people it's
because it has been distorted into becoming a possession: who has power and who hasn't. An institution
that becomes afraid of losing control over people
becomes obsessed with authority, particularly those who
see themselves as having status within that institution.
I'm all too aware how much I collude with such distor-
tions. Education, the drawing out of that which is
within me and is potentially creative, is in danger of
being suffocated in these circumstances. Jesus refuses to
get drawn into a discussion that would become compet-
itive and negative. Most discussions land up with the
same problem.

**Let your heart experience My wisdom that you may
live in My Light.**

THE EXERCISE

The verb 'to discuss' comes from a Latin word meaning 'to shake apart' ['discutere' from 'dis' meaning 'apart' and 'quatere' to shake]. Many discussions are about the airing of prejudices, no matter how clever or intellectual; the desire to win and persuade. The one who listens in a group and asks in-depth questions can have the important task of disturbing the group and shaking it apart. So often, I've participated in a group when I want to impress to win, just for the sake of it. Jesus' question was an attempt to listen to the fears of the chief priests. Listening is the key. If you are in a group of some kind, try to listen to each other and not turn your group work into a contest. Listening involves simply reflecting verbally on what you hear someone else say in the group. In the silence, reflect on conversations in groups that you have had and notice your responses in that group. Remain for a while in the silence and just be content with listening to your own life and breathing.

- - -

104.

THE PILGRIMAGE

I've just tripped on a rock and fallen full-on into a cow pat! Two pilgrims are helping me clear myself up. They say they're pilgrims but then add, rather defensively, that they're not 'believers'. "Why are you making the pilgrimage then?" One of them replies, "Oh. We're intrigued, I suppose, by the process of pilgrimage as a human endeavour." Perhaps they're trying to save my embarrassment. "Is that all that it is for you?" I ask equally defensively. Francis scowls at me. Later he comments, "God bless them for their honesty and their love and care of you. Ubi caritas, Deus ibi est – Where love is, there is God." A question occurs to me, "Well. What's the point of believing then?" Francis smiles and I wince, "Your leg is healing," he says.

Read the section: Matthew 21:28-32

THE REFLECTION

Remember that a parable tends to make one point only. The unlikely ones, for 'religious' people at any rate, by what they do and say appear to refuse the supposed benefits of religion, are the ones who are accepted. I'd do well to be careful about my attitudes not only to people of different faiths, but to those who seem to resist having anything to do with 'religion'. They're saying something to me to which I must listen. Given the history of certain kinds of religious 'righteousness' in this and the last century, it doesn't take much to imply exclusion which in extreme circumstances can lead to ethnic cleansing. Christianity is not about my security, but it's about my insecurity that I'm prepared to live with for the love of the alienated. In summary, prayer, inclusion and compassion.

Open your heart to My Wisdom that sees My Truth in all.

THE EXERCISE

The desire for affirmation is often greater than the desire to do a requested job. It takes some courage to say 'no' to a request sometimes, because it may cause criticism and rejection. My saying 'yes' can so often be about pleasing people. Most jobs, however, need to be done for their own sakes. The ones who actually 'do' the job are often the 'outsiders' because they have less to lose. They probably know that they aren't going to be accepted anyway. In your prayer imagine or remember a caring person you know but who'll have chosen not to be involved in Christianity, or who belongs to a different culture than you. Then look for what is creative in them. You'll see that what they do or don't believe is less significant. What they are and speak of is love and active kindness. Not a bad desire for yourself in your meditation.

- - -

105.

THE PILGRIMAGE

Apart from my little copy of Matthew's Gospel in one pocket, in another, I've a little hand-written collection of poetry. But sadly, with the recent torrential rain, my clothes and the little books are soaked through, again. However, the poetry is wrapped in several layers of cloth. Francis watches me as I put the contents of my pockets out to dry by the fire in our lodgings. "You really value these poems, don't you?" Asks Francis, looking a little surprised. "Yes. I do cherish them". So Francis asks if he can take it to read in his bunk. The following day, I've forgotten about the little book and the rain continues to pour down. As we stop in the ruins of a cottage for shelter, I ask Francis for my poetry. Francis reaches into his bag. "Oh dear! It's soaking again. I'm furious. "Don't worry", says Francis, "I've learnt all the poems by heart. I'll write them out for you." "But you must have spent all night learning them!" But I do miss my book.

Read the section: Matthew 21:33-45

THE REFLECTION

Ownership, possessing property and 'things', is deeply sunk into my psyche, because I identify with them. The fantasy that I have is that they'll give me a way of being that's different from the one I have. Again, I rub up against the dangers of possessiveness ['My Church, 'My beliefs', 'My vocation' or we say 'Our...']. The more importance I give to territory and property, the more I stake it out to defend it. Technology has provided new ways to turn my home into my castle. Christ stands outside those boundaries, that I create, and weeps. Freedom is in danger of becoming less important than being safe. Safety is so often an illusion. At the heart of Christianity is the way of insecurity and uncertainty.

That your heart may be still and aware of My Freedom.

THE EXERCISE

Begin with silence as usual and use the sentence for a good stretch of time. As you may have done before, look at the things, issues and people to which you feel attached. They may be vitally important in and for your life. Use the parable to deepen your imagination. The parable points to the simplicity of cooperating, working with others, indeed with all around you to enrich life and not only yours. Earlier in Matthew's Gospel, Jesus taught about poverty of spirit. Perhaps it's becoming clearer what that means. Letting go of your feelings of possessiveness is hard, of course, and for some, very hard. Renunciation is not the demand here. It 's freedom. Strangely, you will find delight in what things and people you're given to care for but are not yours. And they become even more enjoyable because they're not yours.

- - -

CHAPTER TWENTY TWO –
MATTHEW 22

106.

THE PILGRIMAGE

While I pull out some bread from my bag, Francis produces some squashed tomatoes and a half-eaten apple. Thank you, Francis, very much! Next to us, two men and a women are engaging in malicious gossip. Francis turns to them. "Move on from this self-destructive behaviour". They look puzzled and then annoyed. At least they've stopped their destructive conversation. "As for you", he raises his voice to me, "You enjoyed their gossip". I did! At a crossroads, I stop and break into tears. Francis laughs and gives me some marzipan from a paper bag. "Be ready on all occasions for the presence, the suffering, the death and the resurrection of Jesus", he adds with a wink. "Your point is...?" "If you practice awareness of the Presence of Christ, gossip hasn't any room!" He laughs.

Read the section: Matthew 22:1-14

THE REFLECTION

The ones who are at the crossroads are at least prepared to go in whatever direction they are called. They're waiting. But the waiting to which Christ alludes includes a personal readiness: a waiting on God. So I'm summoned to be at the crossroads and to have all my affairs in order – the wedding garment. The Gospel writers assumed that readers would be familiar with the Kingdom of God being like a banquet, a wedding, a party. After all, the best relationships include eating and celebrating together. Beautifully prepared food is a sign of love that you may have for me as your guest; a sign of being ready to move on in relationships. Once again the Kingdom of God is not static, a place; it's a process, a journey. Perhaps the best parties take place on pilgrimages!

In stillness, let your heart and mind be aware of my call to follow My Way.

THE EXERCISE

If you can, go out for a brief walk with Matthew's Gospel. Notice the simple activities of how you prepare for this walk. Begin by noticing the environment of your walk: the weather, the street, path or pavement, the buildings, the natural world around you. Smell, look, feel. Stop for a few moments, in a safe and, if possible, inconspicuous place, and read the passage above twice. Then as you continue, recall the parable. Return to your place of prayer and use the sentence to deepen your awareness to Christ's vocation and the state of your personal readiness.

- - -

107.

THE PILGRIMAGE

A priest has joined us, with a look on his face which leaves me wondering. Is it arrogance or fear, or both? Arrogance is often a posture adopted by the fearful as an attempt not to have the fear exposed. Francis seems to be have been talking with the priest for hours. As the priest leaves us, I comment, "I noticed that when you asked the priest a question, he had an answer ready." Francis looks sadly as the priest walks into the distance. "When, however, the priest asked you a question, your response was cautious of not knowing, of uncertainty." All Francis says is "Maybe."

Read the section: Matthew 22:15-22

THE REFLECTION

Two groups which represent religion and local politics feel threatened by Jesus. So they hoped by a 'pincer' movement to trap Jesus. Caesar is 'divine', a challenge to the political control of the occupying Romans and in addition, Jesus is a direct challenge to Jewish theology. One is political dissidence and the other for blasphemy. His neat reply is in the form of a riddle. The Kingdom of God is breaking in but it is also not here. All religion falls into the trap of either being over-identified with political power and norms or putting itself beyond them. The motivation for both can be disturbingly similar. The way of Christ demands simplicity. However, true simplicity is delicate and demands a refined balance. And I'm in danger if I ever think I'm going to achieve that balance.

Let the Way of Your Truth deepen my awareness of Your Life in all things.

THE EXERCISE

Though it may not be noticed, by not identifying yourself with the drive for power over others and by refining the spiritual antennae of awareness, you can begin to live and work in the middle of human structures with some freedom, and so bring a simple prophetic insight of detachment, simply by the way you are. This demands great discipline and practice. That's why it's important for you to spend time regularly in the silent prayer of stillness; by dropping down into your inner life. That refined balance is achieved by the Spirit of Christ that then has a consequent effect in your outer life.

- - -

108.

THE PILGRIMAGE

Francis climbs over a wall to give two doleful donkeys something to eat, gathering what he can by digging around beneath the snow. The wind howls through the stone wall. Francis speaks with the donkeys, or rather shouts at them because of the strong wind, trying to console them. Then Francis gathers broken branches to form a better wind-break that the dilapidated wall. In the late evening at an inn, I see that he's wincing. "What's wrong with you?" "Listen to them", Francis whispers. "The murmuring of yet more gossip from two pilgrims that undermines others who aren't present." He holds his cloak in front of them, in effect hiding them from the other guests in the inn. "What are you doing?", I ask. "I'm protecting the guests from the storm blowing from these men's mouths." I laugh, but the men didn't. Later as I'm about to sleep, I hear Francis weeping. "Dear patient Christ, my friend, I too gossip. I too undermine!"

Read the section: Matthew 22:23-33

THE REFLECTION

Being able to win an argument in a debate is a longing of mine; having that smug sense of trapping my opponent, enhancing my ego and reducing the other's.

Worse, often in conversations I show my prowess over another, when that other is not present. Admitting to the desire to undermine someone of whom I'm jealous or afraid is hard. So, the Sadducees desire to trap Jesus is one with which I can identify all too painfully. Every circumstance becomes a creative opportunity for Jesus. So he speaks of 'now', the circumstances and the people in this moment, which is of God. While I may fret about what I do and don't believe, about my own agenda, I miss the opportunity to perceive God's creative desire in and for this moment.

I would receive Your Grace to listen to others as Your Living Presence in the present moment.

THE EXERCISE

Establish silence, using the sentence as a listening to God that becomes more of an attitude that you'll have towards others in your daily life. Silence is not the same as the absence of noise or the refusal to speak or engage. The Carthusians, an order of monks, dedicated to silence write, paradoxically, of their speaking in silences. There are those from whom you may have tried to distance yourself out of fear or dislike. Maybe you've wanted to undermine them in order to protect or inflate your own ego. Maybe you have even made your negative feelings known. See that person in your imagination and ask for the gift of listening. Ask also to be freed from the desire to undermine. What happens, you'll notice, is that gradually you'll see what's true in that person because you're being true to yourself. The desire for ego-inflation becomes redundant. You begin to see it as a waste of energy!

- - -

109.

THE PILGRIMAGE

Matthew's Gospel has been with us both throughout the pilgrimage, but in a way, I feel I've come to know Jesus less and less. Francis has that habit of slapping me on my back when I'm low. "Come on. Snap out of it!" That's so irritating. And, yes, he doesn't seem to become depressed and anxious like me! Many pilgrims seem to gather at various points on the route, to ask him questions and perhaps catch a few of his pearls. Yes, I'm envious! I want that kind of admiration, but I don't let such longings be known. Francis has just said to me, as we set out again, "The worst part of my personality is that I want to hold onto those I've come to love." "But all they want to do is to thank you!" "Precisely! But I want more than that." I enjoy this admission too much.

Read the section: Matthew 22:34-40

THE REFLECTION

The two greatest commandments have a simplicity to them that disturbs me. They've a strong imperative. The whole person must move out to The Otherness of God. In the slip-stream of this movement is the loving of my neighbour. The development of the personal spiritual life happens as a consequence of this attitude and activity. However, my inner life is where the well-spring of The Spirit is. The Love and Service of the other person is almost reflex reaction to my inner life.

Wait still on My Life and My Love that your life may be Christ-like in simplicity and service.

THE EXERCISE

In your meditation, it is important to remember a simple process. You move inwards, in order to move outwards. That's why that pattern is explicit in Christian Liturgy. The Eucharist is a process of moving in to offer the community of faith; the 'Body' to God, then to receive the sacrament, the active sign of God, in order then to move out to give. So, in a sense, all prayer is eucharistic, sacramental. In meditation, you move into the work of praying in order to offer your life in Love to God, with all your distractions, doubts, hope and emptiness. But, remember, you do this with others, even when you're alone. You then move out, while still in meditation, otherwise the meditation bears little or no relationship to the life you're living, let alone loving.

- - -

110.

THE PILGRIMAGE

Francis and I are miserable from being soaked through with driving rain. Knowing that Francis is miserable is strangely reassuring. He trips and falls, putting his right hand out to stop his fall, breaking his wrist. Dancing around, he moans and wails, jumping up and down in agony. I wrap his wrist with a cloth I've been using to keep my Matthew's Gospel dry. "My hand feels as if it's come away from my arm. I'm never going to be able to use it again." Sitting by a blazing fire, he calms down as I help him drink some soup and eat some fresh bread. "How, my good friend, am I going to understand Christ's pain when I can't come to terms with this?" He asks, pathetically. I shrug my shoulders. His question isn't rhetorical, he's begging me for an answer. A deep question from Francis! Humility indeed, hardly pathetic.

Read the section: Matthew 22:41-46

THE REFLECTION

Some first century Jews held that Messiah would be David's son. However, if Messiah is greater than David, there is a difficulty. So Christ is both Son and Lord. In western ways of thinking, I've been imbued with the assumptions of hierarchy, including in Christendom. Jesus plays with this. To be Son is to be in God and to be Lord is to be a slave! So, when I say 'Lord Jesus' I'm turning the meaning of the word 'Lord' upside down. Thus, Jesus puts a question mark over all assumptions about power and indeed about human relationships.

Let Me be your servant that you, being in God, may serve.

THE EXERCISE

Questions and knowing how to ask them, as this pilgrimage has shown, reveal the power of Jesus. Mostly, when questions are asked they demonstrate that one person is dependent on another to answer. So asking a question gives away power. Questions then reveal humility. That's precisely where the 'power' of Christ is: service. So the focus of spirituality is in the inner desire to know, to grow, as has been shown, in order to move outwards to serve. You may have a question for someone today. What lies at the heart of your question? In your silence enter that question then use the sentence. What is the real question in your heart that you want to put to God?

- - -

CHAPTER TWENTY THREE –
MATTHEW 23

111.

THE PILGRIMAGE

Francis has been moaning away that no one has asked for his advice for days. No one has said as much as 'thank you'. "Poor you!", I mockingly add. He turns over on his bunk and snorts. I think I've just heard him swear under his breath! "But Francis, you've spoken about humility being the giving away power." "Yes! I spoke about it. You know by now that it's another matter practicing it." "Well," I reply knowing I'm doing so with more than a note of self-satisfaction, "If it was me saying these things, you'd probably say, 'If you can't live it yourself, then let Christ live it in you.'" He snorts!

Read the section: Matthew 23:1-11

THE REFLECTION

To have some inner acceptance would mean that I wouldn't need to be noticed or concerned about my status. The weaker and more anxious political and religious institutions become, the more names, ranks and hierarchies seem to appear. Jesus makes the assumption that when I follow him I can begin to experience inner acceptance for two reasons. The first is that I acknowledge the Kingdom of God as the only process into which human endeavour is aiming to be incorporated. That process is entirely characterised by service and not power. The second is that God has such prior place in my consideration that status is of little if no significance.

I would be more and more free to be of service to the Hope of Christ.

THE EXERCISE

What you choose to wear, your manner in all conversations, what you spend your resources on, reveal more about you than you probably realise. Self-image is perhaps more important to you than you're prepared to admit. If whole classes or ethnic groups feel resentful about being insecure, there are profound dangers, which our cultures, East and West are now experiencing. On the other hand, to seek for admiration or sympathy or both, for their own sakes is to be cut off from the health of Christ's gift of hope in God. And that gift is called Grace. In the silence, look at recent days and relive the experiences where you sought for attention for its own sake. This exercise is not about guilt, but about becoming awake to motivation and action. In your prayer, ask deeply to have your 'compass bearings' reset to the love and service of God in others.

- - -

112.

THE PILGRIMAGE

A young woman has joined us. Despite her years, her face already shows the marks of pain and anxiety. There's an intensity in her eyes. Francis is sitting on some dry grass and showing the young woman his copy of Matthew's Gospel, describing how he and I have been using Matthew on our pilgrimage. Francis shows, of course, huge knowledge and confidence in the Gospel, but I'm irritated by what seems a self-righteousness in his tone. We become embroiled in a lengthy argument, sounding off about our knowledge and experience in the Way of Christ. The young woman listens intently until, at last, there's a break in our prattle. She speaks quietly, "I wonder, listening to you, how confident you are in The Way. You may have knowledge and experience, I suppose. Isn't the love of God for and in you of much greater significance?" Silence descends. I hope she stays! Or do I?

Read the section: Matthew 23:13-32

THE REFLECTION

"I am one of those who have the key to finding God. To find God, be like me. I give my attention to the things of God rather than God himself. My scrupulosity over the details of my life is designed to impress. I give pride of place to my image of myself. My attention to my outer life is starving my inner life. I blame others for the maltreatment of the saints of the past masking my complicity in violence." These seven adapted 'exposures' within me arise from the Matthew section. Some, if not all of them, make me cringe. The question I have for myself is 'why'. Such self-examination, at the heart of Christian spirituality, has provided the opportunity for self-examination in the early Christian Church to the present day, in order to be clear about the Church's motivation in preparation for God's Kingdom. For me to have a pure motivation is an illusion, but to be aware of that is essential.

I thank you that you are opening my heart to Your Clarity in preparation for living in Your Truth.

THE EXERCISE

Begin with silence and the sentence until you feel still enough to look at this exercise. Use the seven 'exposures' above to review some of your attitudes. If it feels appropriate, write your reactions down honestly without being over-analytical. Don't try at this stage to make any resolutions. Simply observe your feelings that arise and face them for what they are. You may want to share your observations with a spiritual director or someone you trust. Soon the story of the Passion will be the greatest exposure of motivation that there is.

- - -

113.

THE PILGRIMAGE

Francis frequently before sleep, kneels upright for about ten minutes, no matter how tired he is. I made a note some time ago of two striking aphorisms: "Going to sleep is a preparation for death. Prayer is one of constant preparation." With a wry smile he adds that he may die that night, and, looking at me with a bigger smile, "and so might you". In the morning he rises early. After all, the early morning is the time of the rising of Jesus. Francis' habit has become important for me. "Rise and listen to God before anything else preoccupies your consciousness," Francis says repeatedly. He uses his Matthew and his memorised prayers, mostly from the psalms. "Waiting and stillness are the roots of awareness. In these attitudes, I sense the rumour of God. These gifts of Christ are not what I or indeed you may do. They're gifts of God." "But after that, what do I do?" I ask feeling stupid. "Let yourself be in the present moment to receive these gifts. Obedience, my friend!"

Read the section: Matthew 23:33-39

THE REFLECTION

The genius of Judaism is that intimacy with God is in all human activity. Yes, all, because that's where I encounter the Love of God; the focus of every moment of my life. When religious institutions behave otherwise, there's a denial not only of God but what it is to be human and a responsible participant in creation. Political schemes that denied the inspiration of God had corrupted Jerusalem inspired civic life, centred on the presence of God. The prophets were those who drew attention to denial, sometimes in dramatic ways that lead to their rejection and in many cases elimination by the leaders of religious institutions. That disturbing process is as much if not a major cultural issue for me now.

Realise in your heart that I am the Source of Life in all you are and do.

THE EXERCISE

This meditation is best practiced at the end of the day; preferably before you are too tired! Sit or kneel in silence and use the sentence to focus your mind into your heart. Then review each detail of your day. What were the priorities that governed your attitudes and your behaviour? Recall the various points during the day when you can perceive God's presence and his will for you. In the morning, midday and the evening, a simple form of prayer, reading of the bible and of great men and women who have travelled with the presence of God, can help you maintain your spiritual centre. With someone you know who is experienced, you'll get advice about this that matches your life and responsibilities. I would add that for Christians this discipline of prayer is an obligation, perhaps not a word that sits well with a culture obsessed with 'choice' and trivialised notions of freedom.

– – –

CHAPTER TWENTY FOUR –
MATTHEW 24

114.

THE PILGRIMAGE

Francis is looking pale and tired. There's a little dwelling just off the path, with smoke rising from the almost discernible chimney; a welcoming sight. The little old man takes us in, giving us some water to wash ourselves. He produces soup and bread. There by the fire are four other pilgrims. Three of them are watching and listening to the fourth with awe. After a while one of them asks Francis: "Do you not know that you're in the presence of a great spiritual teacher? His knowledge of the scriptures is astounding." Francis simply says, "I'm enjoying my soup. That's enough spirituality for me just now." Later I comment, "You can be rude, d'you know?" His answer was enigmatic. "Beware of spiritual teachers, particularly great ones." "Does that include you?" I ask cheekily. "Especially me!"

Read the section: Matthew 24:1-14

THE REFLECTION

Jerusalem was sacked in 70CE and the writer of the Gospel was probably feeding back that experience into

Jesus' sayings. In my reading of this passage, I'm having my compass bearings readjusted. The Kingdom of God is beyond any temporary civilisation or political system. Fear is engendered when a status quo or 'my' life is under threat. By focusing on God's Kingdom my fears then become redundant. When there's fear of collapse on any scale, characters emerge in public who claim apocalyptic insights and powers for themselves and a myriad of groups dominated by autocratic personalities particularly in the world of spirituality and religion, played out in the realms of religious 'righteousness' as well as fantasy and, inevitably, effective marketing.

Be still and know the Truth of My Kingdom within that frees you from fear.

THE EXERCISE

What makes it difficult for you to 'name' your fears, even to yourself? Do you recognise inclinations in yourself to shift responsibility for your fears on to something or somebody else? Who do you know that accepts you for who you are and you can speak to about your fears? When you look at a well-known Christian leader that you admire, what qualities does he or she have? So in the silence allow your fear to come to the surface, but do so keeping the sentence as the main focus.

- - -

115.

THE PILGRIMAGE

Two fit-looking girls join us. They're covered in mud and soaked, but they're blissfully happy. "We've been asking about you and Francis for many days, hoping to meet you. And here you are!" Straight away, I wax eloquent on Matthew's Gospel, that I'm carrying in my pocket. "I've got it in my heart now", I add, perhaps with false certainty in the Kingdom of God and how they might have the same. Francis, who's walking just ahead of me, turns and glowers at me. "And are you ready to be crucified? Only then claim that you're anywhere near knowing the Kingdom. Perhaps then, God in whom you claim to be certain, will be come a matter of doubt and love." Does Francis really need to embarrass me?

Read the section: Matthew 24:15-28

THE REFLECTION

Religious communication around the first century CE was often portentous. This was not surprising, given the Roman occupation, the interplay of many religious cultures in the Near East; and then the destruction of Jerusalem in 70CE. Matthew's Gospel was probably written not long after that devastating experience. Currently, when there's uncertainty about the future and even the survival of our own culture, there are many political and religious leaders who attract attention to themselves, manipulating the emotions and fears of many. One of the distorting marks of religious pros-elytism is its self-generated certainty. And certainty I find tempting when I feel anxious about the future. Religious certainty is often presented as being based on faith in God. This kind of certainty, like a hovering vulture, is inclined to feed off the fearful. Jesus, it's true, had a prophetic sense of the terrifying implications and consequences of 'world' affairs as he knew them, but implored that those who followed him take responsib-ility for themselves and be constantly prepared for God's kingdom and not be distracted by the oppor-tunism of fanatics. And that applies to me!

Let your heart and mind be awake to My Wisdom.

THE EXERCISE

Jesus didn't condemn fear, despite the fact that he fre-quently exclaimed: 'Do not be afraid'. Everyone is afraid of something at some point. Indeed, in some cir-cumstances, fear is essential in order to avoid harmful and dangerous outcomes. Christ was simply acknow-ledging the power of fear. What matters is to recognise and understand your fears, as you experience them physically and psychologically in this moment. This understanding is one of the creative emphases to arise out of the considerable interest in Mindfulness. The

outcome will gradually be that your fears will have less
and less power over you. You'll find that you begin to
focus on what's really important. You'll be less prone to
being imprisoned by your fears and by those who use
fear for their own desire for power. So, begin your meditation by looking at that of which you are afraid. Don't
try and get rid of fears or chastise yourself for having
them. Have compassion on yourself. Move into praying
gently with the sentence. Once or twice during the day,
when fears rear their heads, use the sentence and just
notice how your fears operate in you. Ask God that
your fears may be used for others healing: a preparation
for the Kingdom of God.

- - -

116.

THE PILGRIMAGE

Francis talks of the importance of praying in silence
early in the morning, before intrusions break in. "But,
remember intrusions and even the most trivial distraction indicate the movement of God. Come to think
of it, I'm not sure I like those words intrusions and distractions when we're talking about prayer." This
morning, however, Francis eyes are sunken and he looks
anxious. "Francis?" I ask nervously. "You look pale and
anxious." As he turns to me, he looks like a desperate

child to my eyes. "I'm lost. I simply can't pray."
"Why?" I ask gently. "Because I'm constantly con-
fronted by my fear of dying and death, of loneliness.
Sometimes confidence in the Love of God deserts me".
Is this the real Francis speaking? Inwardly, I smile at the
honesty, strength in weakness. This is holiness indeed!

Read the section: Matthew 24:29-36

THE REFLECTION

Three strands of Jewish culture and belief come
together. To be honest, I've always found these difficult
to grasp. But I can try. One strand is the well-established hope and belief that there would be an 'ideal
man', one who would be utterly obedient to God as
servant and prophet. The second strand was a
developed sense that the end of all things would not be
the end for God. All events in creation were God-
events, including devastation and suffering. The third
strand was that this 'man' is effective in bringing
healing and love —redemption – even in the course of
the 'end' breaking in. Jesus for Christianity became the
coming together, the focus of these strands: The Son of
man. Are you clearer? Perhaps not. Does it matter?
Well, hope does. Hope deepens love.

**Let the eyes of your heart be open to my Healing and
my Love in all creation and experience.**

THE EXERCISE

In the face of many destructive images in the news media, in the suffering of someone you love or maybe your own suffering, it's difficult, if not impossible, to discern God's healing and loving. For some of you, perhaps, the stomach tenses; the heart races and the dark clouds of depression gather; or all three. Praying in the middle of anxiety and depression is hard. That's because just getting through ordinary life becomes hard. Maybe, in praying, you can only last a minute, if that! It's in these moments, no matter how brief, that prayer is of vital importance. Don't concern yourself as to whether you're concentrating or not. Acknowledge briefly that God is to found in all your experiences – yes – all. Simply use the sentence faithfully throughout the day and you will begin to see God as the one at the heart of all your experiences. Not that you'll necessarily feel any better, but just sticking with how you actually are in your praying may be of vital importance to you and to others.

- - -

117.

THE PILGRIMAGE

A young woman has been walking in silence, for a few miles, with Francis. I'm trying to be silent too. It helps that I've got a chest infection and I've lost my voice. My breathing's difficult, affecting my sleep as well as walking. We've stopped for some bread, cheese and some fruit, so I ask the young woman, in a whisper, "Why haven't you been saying much to Francis, let alone asking him any questions?" "I've been trying to learn from him how to watch and to listen." "But, there's been no conversation to listen to", I add. "Yes, there has. I'm listening to the silence and that brings up its own questions." What was she talking about? Francis smiles at me. "Remember, silence is the gift of God. It's not the absence of sound. It's a divine gift of simplicity. And in explaining that to you, I have said too much!"

Read the section: Matthew 24:37-44

THE REFLECTION

Jesus was not so much concerned with the actual events of a devastating end to history. The fact that it, or simply my own death can happen at any time ['momento mori'], calls for constant awareness. The speculations of enthusiasts for apocalyptic events also distracts me from the crucial issues of 'this' moment.

There are other lives I can watch and listen to:, those who have lived a life of simplicity; who have followed a vocation, have chosen to be poor in order to be awake, to however the presence of God is to be discerned in 'this' moment. Now.

I would have my life simplified by the indwelling Spirit of awareness of Your call to me in each moment.

THE EXERCISE

The difficulty of possessions keeps on arising in the Gospel. Being aware of it is worth repeating. Look around your room now. How encumbered are you by 'things'? The vocation is to be ready and awake enough to discern God's presence in your life and the lives of others. What gets in the way of that? Can you do something about it? Seek guidance from a spiritual director of skill otherwise this exercise can be nothing other than a plunge into guilt. On the other hand, you can easily avoid such uncomfortable questions. However, some 'things' are for sheer enjoyment. They can be means of discerning God's presence. The issue is whether you are free to have them or not to have them. It's identifying yourself as 'possessing' them that can be the disease. Use the sentence to deepen this awareness.

- - -

CHAPTER TWENTY FIVE –
MATTHEW 25

118.

THE PILGRIMAGE

We can't find any inn with bunks because the whole town's full of wedding guests. And I want a bunk, because I want a good night's sleep. How I dislike that forced cheerfulness of wedding guests. Nevertheless, we've been invited to attend the wedding. Outside the church, in the square there's wonderful food and dancing. I notice the bride coming across to Francis, sitting on the wall surrounding the village fountain. She spots Francis' little copy of the gospel of Matthew on his lap. "What do you carry that for?" she asks dismissively. "Well, for the same reason as you might carry it with you everywhere. Christ's summoning you to live like him in your marriage, and he loves weddings, remember." "I'm not interested in this religious stuff." She speaks with a sneer. "Hear me out," urges Francis. "In marriage, you can learn to be a servant and maybe to suffer on behalf of the one you love. This will lead you to be a servant and to carry the suffering of many." There's a change in her attitude. "Yes," Francis speaks quietly to her, almost in her ear, "Christ in you. Try it." I wonder what's happened to her.

Read the section: Matthew 25:1-13

THE REFLECTION

There's no getting away from it, but I find this hard. On the one hand, I'm presented with a picture of suffering and on the other hand I'm invited to imagine a party! In the Old Testament, the prophets guided, cajoled and even brow-beat the Hebrews into seeing that God's love, both terrifying as well as tender, were behind even the catastrophic events of their history. Messiah, a servant-leader, would bring the people into a new way of trust in God, through suffering and service. Jesus was, in the Gospel of Matthew, the realisation of that hope. And so, with Jesus there would always be endings, which would be part of God's creation and recreation history. Hence in Matthew, acute readiness for the presence of Christ is central. The story about the wedding attendant chimed with a well-established tradition that living in union with God would be like a wedding banquet: the intensification of loving, serving relationships in the context of delight.

Let the Hope of bringing you into Union with Me, enrich your heart for serving Me in each moment.

THE EXERCISE

Despite the fact that many marriages don't work out, nevertheless there still lingers the hope that marriage will somehow be a delightful union and a metaphor for eternity. This is symbolised in the giving and receiving of rings at a wedding. The Christ of this moment summons you to be attentive to the potential for union. The tragedy is that the more awake you are, the more you'll realise how many opportunities you've missed for delight and realising God's presence in union, which is, if you like, an intimate friendship. So empathise with the foolish wedding attendants! As you move into silence look at the last twenty four hours and become aware of the opportunities that you've used in the most insignificant circumstances. With the sentence, move into the detail and allow God to intensify his union within you.

- - -

119.

THE PILGRIMAGE

A young boy has joined us, and I notice that his parents are walking a good distance behind us. The boy has heard that I sing and wants to accompany me on his flute. "You're too good for me; I'd probably spoil your playing," I reply with barely believable humility. But then Francis sings instead: out of tune! "Come on," he barks at me. "Don't be so precious. Sing!" Soon, we're joined by about twenty people laughing and singing. I'm feeling resentful and humiliated. So I drop out and hang behind. The singing and laughter doesn't stop.

That night, Francis scowled at me and told me to read a story from Matthew.

Read the section: Matthew 25:14-30

THE REFLECTION

The most important part of this parable is where the third servant had hidden the talent given him: "...so I was afraid." Yes, it's my old friend fear again! Now I find it easy to forget that parables only make one main point. And there, my attention's drawn away from the single-hearted focus of our life to the Kingdom of God. What I realise is that another way of describing the challenge of the gospel is the matter of identity. Giving my attention to the Kingdom, I'll be less and less identified with human solutions or power structures. Fear, as revealed in this passage, demonstrates the power I've given to others. In turn, the decisions I find myself making are to placate or even to appease. So, I become more interested in pleasing those in power rather than loving God from the experience of being loved.

Let me be aware of the gifts you have given me and so offer them in Your service for others.

THE EXERCISE

Read the passage carefully and slowly several times. Then imagine that Jesus is telling you the story. He's with you now. What do you do in your daily life to focus on the will of God for you? What do you do to please or placate others out of fear? Write down your reactions to this question. Then quickly write down the gifts you have and then let the sentence drop down into your silence and stillness. Imagine you have your gifts in the palms of your hands, given to you to honour and to use. Note your feelings.

- - -

120.

THE PILGRIMAGE

"Do you know what has tired me most?" Francis ruminates almost plaintively. There's no point in me saying anything in reply, because he's going to tell me anyway. "I've been carrying in my heart, on the pilgrimage, those for whom I've been asked to pray. I feel, for example, a powerlessness in praying for two factions back home, who've been at war with each other for decades with no prospect of peace. There's the awful sense of Christ's Gospel demand that the Church be one in Christ, and yet animosity, suspicion and the desire for power and influence are deep within the Body of Christ. And there's awful poison, not losing face." As he creeps into his bunk, he weeps, hoping I won't notice. I realise that here's the intercession of Christ being lived out in this little holy man. In some strange way, he's a sign of hope. His holiness feels like an exposure on my resentments and divisions. His holiness is based on the simplest fact, he's obedient to the call to follow Jesus, no more, no less. 'The End' of all things will surely be marked by such love.

Read the section: Matthew 25:31-46

THE REFLECTION

In the Old Testament, the development of a concept of 'the end of all things' comes through the experience of suffering and catastrophic events, laying out the way God communicates with his people: a judging of us. The focus of this development is often on a single figure: The 'Son of man'. This mythological character's of huge moral and spiritual stature, who'll suffer at the hands of humanity's distorting behaviour and will judge humanity at the 'end'. The word mythological does not mean that the Son of Man is not real, but that there isn't an adequate factual way to describe the image 'Son of Man'. As the title suggests, although there's an exalted tone to it, nevertheless there is a sense in the texts that the Son of Man is also a representational figure. Therefore, I'm caught up in the movement towards the end now. Matthew's Gospel makes the connection between Jesus and the 'Son of man' image; the realisation of the image, as it were. The use of the title in Jesus calls me to waken up to the urgent need to change my life-style as a preparation for the 'end', because as the Son of man is identified with Jesus then the end is not far away. Indeed, that 'end' is breaking-in now. So, there is injected into me a sense of urgency about following Jesus, provided I don't take myself too seriously. The Passion and Resurrection of Christ is the exposure of the very presence of the Son of man.

Be still and know the freeing power of My Wisdom within you.

THE EXERCISE

The rise of anxiety over the ecology of the planet, the delicacy of global economics, coupled with the perpetual threat of nuclear or bio-chemical warfare has raised awareness of 'the end'. Indeed, you may feel, and not unjustifiably so, that you must take some responsibility for these outcomes, no matter how minimally. However, the Gospel summons you to be awake to this moment as an 'end'. After all, your own death, as has been suggested, could happen at any moment. So in this exercise, imagine your own death, but you may want to do so with someone with whom you can share the exercise. What happens a few moments before your death? What happens at your death, then just afterwards: to your body, to your belongings, to those you love? Repeat the same, but move down say ten years or twenty or forty, even a hundred and so on. Using the sentence after this exercise is a powerful experience of waking up to this moment! However, again, you might want to have company for this exercise, as it might well raise feelings and reactions with which you need support.

- - -

CHAPTER TWENTY SIX – MATTHEW 26

122.

THE PILGRIMAGE

Two young men, dressed in military uniform, shout at us. "Move to the side and let the procession pass!" Five minutes later, important officials pass with that air of pride and power. Francis smiles at it all, while I'm resentful. "Do you notice what really lies behind their masks?" "But, they don't seem to notice that you, Francis, are here, right next to them." I suppose that rises from my desire for reflected glory. But it's not happening. In the inn, the officials are surrounded by those in the local community who want to be seen among them, including, of course, church leaders. Francis approaches them and puts down his copy of Matthew's Gospel on the table in front of them. One well-dressed official looks at Francis and signals Francis to remove the grubby little book. Francis asks them gently: "Have you read this? Have you ruminated with the Gospel? Have you prayed with it? Have you rested with it?" There's both awkwardness and contempt in the church leaders faces. Inside me, there's both anger and fear. Francis sees this straight away and puts his hand on mine. "Do not meet fear with fear!" "How do you know I'm afraid?" "It's in your eyes: that combination of envy of those in power and resentment that you don't have it. The power you've already been given, you're forgetting. This room is charged with self-importance. And I can feel it rising in myself!" Again, I'm astonished by the honesty of this little man.

Read the section: Matthew 26.1-5

THE REFLECTION

The three days of Jesus' Passion is dove-tailed with prophecy from the Old Testament, which had developed a theology of God's presence to be found in all things. Jesus himself was aware of the political processes that would lead to his execution. Religious leaders have always felt threatened by those who have a spirituality that's immediate and who raise questions about institutions that protect their own power base and vested interests. I can almost smell the anxiety of the chief priests and elders; that terrifying prospect of loss of control that I recognise in myself.

Let My Freedom within you lead you to a deeper awareness of My Love in others.

THE EXERCISE

When there's a feeling that your own leaders have not been true to their responsibilities, feelings can become critical and be expressed sometimes severely. Look what happens so often in families when a parent dies and the will is read as a record of who's loved; who deserves and those who are left out. The feelings can be intensely destructive, creating divisions, some of which hadn't been recognised or admitted before. But Matthew and the early Church learnt by their acute spirituality to look at their Jewish leaders through the eyes of Christ. Look over recent days and see when and where you've felt threatened and fearful. Was it the possibility of rejection? The loss of control? Use the sentence to look at the detail of your feelings through the eyes of Christ. This challenging exercise can give birth to a more compassionate approach to those with whom you differ and from whom you may even be divided.

- - -

123.

THE PILGRIMAGE

Francis is exhausted and I'm worried. Arriving at a little cottage, the owner, an old lady, offers us water to wash ourselves. Francis is too tired for that, but, frankly, he stinks. "Well then. You wash me." I'm embarrassed into silence! Francis makes me feel even worse. "I'll wash your feet and your head and hair." A laugh nervously. "When you were a boy", he asks, "Did your father or mother not bathe you all over." "Of course", I answer, my mouth now dry. "Well, I am your child now. Wash me all over." Outside behind a barn, Francis strips off as I pour water over him, wash him with a cloth and dry him with what passes for a towel. I keep looking around to see whether anyone's watching, scared of what people might think. But I wouldn't let Francis do the same for me. Lying down on my blanket to sleep, I bury my head, turning away from Francis so that I don't face the intimacy.

Read the section: Matthew 26:6-13

THE REFLECTION

The skin-disease of Jesus' host was probably contagious. It would have been seen as a moral 'sentence', not unlike leprosy. Then, for Jesus, it was risky and even alarming to have a woman be physically intimate with him. Further, the oil was expensive. Lavishing it on Jesus seemed to contradict Jesus teaching about poverty. To cap it all, Jesus used this anointing to prepare his disciples, men and women, for his death, his burial. Of course, anointing was associated with death. Surely, the disciples thought, Jesus death wasn't imminent. It's one thing not to be ready for my own death; but it's also worth reflecting on how little I'm ready for the death of someone I love. With me, I may be saying that I'm not ready for your death. My own agenda is a priority. Jesus has been called The 'Sign of Contradiction', that question-mark that lies over all of our assumptions not least about living and dying. It seems tantamount to an impossibility to get Jesus' disciples to face not only his death but their own. And that resistance is so strong in me. Here again, Jesus goes against the grain. Why? Because his kingdom is not of this 'world'.

I would look for the signs of Your Kingdom in among the rejected.

THE EXERCISE

In your silence, recollect a time when physically you have been loved, in whatever way; some act of love given freely, entirely for you, no matter how small. You'll probably find that you have little feelings of that love that bring the act into the present moment. Get into the detail and enjoy it. It is Eucharistic! 'Do this in remembrance of (anamnesis - recollecting) me.' 'This is my body. This is my blood.' Now recollect some intimate act of love you have given for someone else, particularly to someone most people would reject. Again, perhaps little feelings will come into the present from your act of loving, almost as if you're loving in 'this' moment and not just when it happened. Now, extend this exercise. Imagine someone you're inclined to reject and then – love them! When you consider your own death, it's vital that you do so in the context of being loved and also in your loving, despite how small and inconsequential you feel the loving to be. Use the sentence to deepen your prayer.

- - -

124.

THE PILGRIMAGE

For two days now, a woman with a haunted look has been walking with us; asking Francis questions about his spiritual life. But she's not asking me! Plagued by emotional surges of anxiety in prayer, she asks Francis how she might cope with them. "I think I know what you mean. Let me tell you about my experiences and see whether they match yours." My attempt to put in something from my approach to prayer and the emotions, is ignored by them both! So I stump off on in a silent rage, about which I can do nothing. As we begin walking again, I find myself with the same woman and telling her about Francis' temper and how depressed he can get. "Yes. I can understand why you want to draw on Francis' experience and his obvious holiness, but he has his weaknesses, you know. You should hear him when he's in a bad mood. What a temper!" "Why are you telling me this?" she asked. She saw straight through me.

Read the section: Matthew 26:14-25

THE REFLECTION

The Gospels don't give much detail as to Judas' motivation. One possibility is that he was trying to force Jesus' hand to take on the religious and political powers and bring in the kingdom immediately, about which Jesus frequently spoke. After all, it seemed to Judas that Jesus saw the Kingdom as being very near, not just in terms of it being present but also in time. Judas' other motivation may have been that he was jealous of some of the disciples being closer to Jesus than he was. Perhaps he was frightened that eventually not only Jesus would be arrested but that he would be. A terrible moment of fearful jealousy within me can so easily lead to me destroying the very source of love that has given me life. The feast of Passover provided a possible timing for the realisation of all these motivations. The exposure of betrayal while eating together at table is significant, because it's often an intimate experience. My betraying of someone is paradoxically most destructive and is inclined to happen in my close relationships. Whatever the motivation, Judas' fear is plain to see. So is mine in my betraying.

Let Your Light expose and heal the fear that lies in the depths of my heart.

THE EXERCISE

Jealousy, as I've tried to show, is one of the most dangerous of human emotions. You not only want what someone else has, but you want to make sure the other person can't have it either or worse, you set out to destroy what the other person has or is about to have. It's dangerous because it's a short distance then towards that destructive behaviour affecting the lives of others and not just what they have. In this exercise, as with so many others, you may find it helpful to have someone you trust to talk through your experiences. Recollect the occasion you wanted to behave destructively towards someone. You may feel that you have betrayed that person! Relive the events in detail but don't get caught in that habit of analysing your thoughts and feelings. Despite the difficult subject, the exercise is pointless unless you have compassion on yourself. Now, imagine yourself at table with Jesus and feel the same feelings towards him! However, for the major part of your meditation use the sentence to realise that all these feelings are in you and that you are being freed from them. Christ accepted Judas betraying kiss, he didn't reject it. You are loved even in your betrayal.

- - -

125.

THE PILGRIMAGE

The village at the bottom of the valley lies just below a rough cart track that we seem to have been walking on for days. As we draw closer, smoke creeps stealthily into the still morning sky. Francis, sits on the damp grass at the side of the path, eating some dried fruit and gazing on the uncared for roof of a little house. After resting, we enter the village, with its little equally uncared for chapel, snug among the cottages. However, we find that the door's open with flickering candle-light within. Old women, children and bored looking men lurk in the shadows, waiting. The priest enters and mutters his way through saying mass. But then, as if he's waking up, he says slowly "This is my body", raising his hands with bread between his fingers. Francis and I look at each other, knowing what we're saying to each other. He's here! Christ does, after all, walk with us. "Give us this day our daily bread".

· Read the section: Matthew 26:26-29

THE REFLECTION

In the heart and mind of the Gospel writer, as had been suggested, is the imminent death of Jesus. A meal, ordinary though it would seem from the description, was and is of ultimate significance: Christ, Messiah, Son of Man, the revelation, or realisation of God is in the bread and wine. From this eating and drinking would follow Christ's death. By my participation in this, my eating and drinking, this too becomes part of me. And so, in the food of God and the 'death' of God, there's the route to the activity of the Kingdom that's coming.

In the presence of Your Body and Blood, I would know the mystery of Your Life and Your Death.

THE EXERCISE

The Eucharist, the Thanksgiving offering of Christ's body and blood, isn't simply an act of remembering, it's recollecting, as I've mentioned before: a bringing into the present the Jesus Christ of the Gospel; an enactment of the feast of the Kingdom which is both here and is to come. Heaven and earth truly touch in the Eucharist. The finite is met with the Infinite God of Love. All prayer emanates from this enacted recollection. So, AT imagine that Christ shares bread and wine with you as a table and makes sure you look at him as he says 'This is my body and blood...for you'. From this prayer, you're called to see Christ's Body around you, that you may serve and love wherever and in whoever you see that Body.

- - -

126.

THE PILGRIMAGE

I've just asked Francis where and when the pilgrimage will end. "Ah! Now you're asking. When we come to complete it, it'll be another dying!" I'm close to fed-up with these what seem to me to be cryptic comments. Perhaps stupidly, I add: "Come on! You're so much stronger now. What is it with you: this dying? You're young enough. Death? You're nowhere near it." Francis draws five circles on the soil at the side of the path. Two circles clockwise (The Old and New Testaments) and three anti-clockwise (The Trinity – Father, Son and Holy Spirit). He then winks at me as he says the Lord's Prayer: "Our Father...", holding up the three middle fingers of his right hand, silently pointing at the sun: praying the Resurrection. Francis again showing his love for using symbolic acts. "Soon", he says smiling. Does he mean his death or the end of the pilgrimage, or both? That evening in the inn, I turn to a fellow-pilgrim and wax eloquent that I'm being taught spiritual secrets by Francis. But Francis overhears. "Dying? is that really a secret? Pay attention!" That's me told – again!

Read the section: Matthew 26:30-35

THE REFLECTION

The writer of the Gospel had the Psalms and the Prophets in his blood-stream. He would see the echoes of Jesus' story going back to ringing but disturbing passages in the Old Testament. As I pray with this passage, I'm wrapped up in the experience of the early church perception of Christ both wounded and risen which lies at the source of every part of the Gospel. Christian art, at its best, always shows the risen Christ to be the wounded Christ. This is of ultimate significance. The most alienated and apparently least likely to be associated with the Glory of God, are the very ones through whom I experience the mystery of the Resurrection. Peter, who was to become the founding apostle of the Church, is in the dark as to the significance of this mystery. All his securities are collapsing around him. Therefore he responds out of fear by falling into the trap of ingratiating the one he admires. Oh! I can feel that because I've done it!

That in the alienated, I may affirm the work of Thy Rising.

THE EXERCISE

The psychology of trying to please someone may arise from a natural admiration of that person's skills or personality. The motivation, however, may be your desire to be included in the admired person's life. It may also

be that understandably you want to avoid your weaknesses being exposed. In this exercise, imagine someone
you have come to know and admire. Notice even the
slightest inclination in you to ingratiate. Remember
none of these exercises are about self-accusation. Simply
be aware; notice. Then read the passage again. Identify
with Peter, hearing Jesus speaking to you; understanding the depths of you. Jesus is not a hero or
celebrity to be ingratiated. He is too deeply within you,
for fantasies about his remote otherness to have any
meaning. Francis' five circles prayer is an approach to
using symbols in prayer that you'll find in the Celtic
practice known as 'Chaim'. You can use it outside,
being careful not to look directly into the sun, assuming
it's shining! Return to the Pilgrimage narrative of this
section and practice it yourself. If you come across an
ancient standing cross, it's a powerful experience to
practice it there.

- - -

127.

THE PILGRIMAGE

This pilgrimage is nearly over. What's next in my life?
There are circumstances back home which I'd forgotten
until recently. In an earlier part of the pilgrimage, a
fellow pilgrim had brought me news that my own

region is suffering from starvation and disease. Here am I on pilgrimage while those that I love are suffering and perhaps even resentful that I'm in relatively easy circumstances. To be honest, I'm afraid of returning home. So, yes, I ask Francis: "Has the pilgrimage become an escape for me?" "Perhaps some of it has. Having an escape is important from time to time. When you're tired, you need rest. When you are in pain, you need some medical help to reduce the pain. These are escapes, in a sense." "But do you think that this pilgrimage, any pilgrimage, is something of an evasion." "Ah!" He replied with a knowing look.

Read the section: Matthew 26:36-46

THE REFLECTION

In recent productions of the Oberammergau Passion play, there were two scenes that I found almost too painful to watch. The first was Jesus with his intimate friends in the Garden of Gethsemane and the second was, of course, the Crucifixion. Any comparison between the two would be absurd. However, the agonising sense of abandonment in the Garden in the play had a depth of agony that I hadn't really acknowledged before. 'My soul is sorrowful to the point of death' is one of the sayings of Christ in this scene, that I tend to avoid. To come so close to death because of the intensity of sorrow, perhaps the pressure on Jesus' heart was getting to dangerous levels. The clenched teeth of excruciating agony can almost be felt as he cries for the cup that he has to drink to pass by. This scene of Jesus' agony does not tell us of the conquering of fear. Rather, fear and dread are quite simply faced.

That You may be aware of My Presence in your deepest moments of anguish.

THE EXERCISE

Fear and anxiety, reveal the most vulnerable part of the human psyche. Sometimes I try to avoid being seen to be fearful, as it so often comes with the other fear of being perceived as weak. And so, fear can not only be intensely painful but also an isolating experience. One reaction is to fight; to come out punching. Another reaction is to run away somehow. Fight or flight. The difficulty is that to run away from fear is to assume wrongly that you can leave it behind. The third reaction is to stand and acknowledge it. You're feeling is what it is. Accept it. Neither fight nor flight. This can be perhaps the most important moment of crisis in any inner life. The meditation sentence assumes the 'voice' of the Christ who knows desolation, is offered so that the fear you experience can be faced. But, again, you would be well-advised to share it with someone who is a spiritual director or a listener whom you trust.

- - -

128.

THE PILGRIMAGE

After all these months on this pilgrimage, I've finally realised that he isn't mine – my pilgrimage. That, at least, is one advantage of making it with Francis. There were moments along the way, when my desire for Francis' love [or was it affirmation?], he saw through and I thought I had learnt my lesson. But, now I'm so disappointed in myself that I still feel that Francis' love is not just for the pilgrims we've met, but will be for the myriad pilgrims down history long after I'm dead and forgotten. No wonder I'm having a sleepless night, with this fear of losing what security I had with Francis and the sense of direction he is giving me still. Maybe it's pathetic, but I want him to be recognised as Francis' close friend. After all, am I not the one who made it possible for him to be sought after on this pilgrimage? Tonight, he looks at me across the table while we're finishing the meal and says: "I love you and that love is for you to give away, not to suffocate!" A sting in the tail! He stands up, shakes his head and sits by the fire. At last, I'm beginning to learn that my self-critical feelings are in me. A simple self-acceptance and self-compassion I'll practice.

Read the section: Matthew 26:47-56

THE REFLECTION

The pain that this passage causes me comes from my identifying with both responses. The first is betrayal. Perhaps I'll only betray the one whom I love. That's why Judas' betrayal includes the important detail of the kiss! Betrayal is a form of poisonous resentment, a hatred that my own deep love doesn't bring about the relationship that I want. That kind of love in me wants to define and control love for my own insecurity. To fall in love with someone and then realise that that love is not solely mine, but is part of others' lives as well, can lead to poisonous resentment, destructive of both me and the one I love. The second response, with which I can identify, is the violent reaction of the follower, who drew a sword to defend Jesus. I can almost see and feel the pursed lips and aggressive postures. Jesus sees through both of my responses and allows himself to be abandoned into the hands of those who really want to destroy him, including mine!

Come to Me in your moments of abandonment and realise My Love for you there.

THE EXERCISE

You may dislike someone whom you're acquainted with, but you can't hate someone you haven't loved. In the silence of your prayer, in the presence of Christ, relive in your memory the occasion when you perhaps hated someone, even if it was only for a moment. If you've never hated anyone, then perhaps you're fortunate, or perhaps it's too painful to acknowledge. So, this exercise can be demanding and costly. If you can, look at the history of the destructive relationship and how it moved from delight to poison, perhaps even oscillating between them several times. With Christ, allow the silence and his acceptance of you to heal deeply. Now, one visit to this relationship will not necessarily heal the hurt within you. You may want or feel the urge to return to it. However, again, only do so with someone you trust and then you can share this spiritual and psychological process. This in itself is a pilgrimage.

- - -

129.

THE PILGRIMAGE

There's a headwind, but it's making the walking exhilarating as well as tiring. I've been waiting on Francis by a stile for well over an hour and I'm concerned. Accompanied by five men, he eventually appears with his head bowed as the men shout at him. "You're a waster. You've been on this pilgrimage for months," they bawl, "and attract all these followers of yours, expecting us to feed you out of our poverty. Go on. Move on from

here, and take that useless friend of yours. Scroungers!"
Francis looks at them and says gently, "You're not poor.
Why do you speak on behalf of those who are? What
are you frightened of?" They walk off almost breathless
from the sheer gall of Francis. "How do you cope with
that bullying?" "The practice of prayer is about
attention, practicing as much constant attention as you
can: that attention to the life of the Gospel in this and
every moment within you. With that in your heart,
whatever bullying happens, becomes a matter of irrel-
evance." I should know by now that he always has a
smart answer. Is he that calm? I wonder.

Read the section: Matthew 26:57-68

THE REFLECTION

This is one of those classic Gospel scenes where what's
not said is of the greatest significance. Fear again is a
major feature, submerging the truth under the cloak of
religious and political righteousness.   Righteousness
technically is about being in the 'right' relationship with
God. The word, as I've tried to show, is too frequently
distorted into signifying that it's the preserve of the religious, as well as the politically powerful. Christ was
afraid, but he behaves out of the truth of what he's
thinking and feeling. To accept that Christ was fearful,
I find, isn't easy to accept. At the simplest level, the
brave are not fearless. Bravery arises from facing fear.
To deny fear is to turn away from God who loves in

and through the bleakness of fear. Jesus can see the fear of the Sanhedrin, who feel they must annihilate this perceived religious threat. And in doing so, he engages with the silence of God. Fear is in Peter, who wanted to see what the end would be. The agonising beauty of this part of the gospel isn't to be found in avoidance, but in those fragile moments of powerlessness in Christ's Passion. That's when the Christian Church fulfils its vocation, when I, in that Body of Christ, with you, live and breathe out of powerlessness. I'm tempted to drop the word righteousness!

I would be still with the silence and beauty of God that loves in the middle of fear.

THE EXERCISE

There are countless ways of using this section of Matthew for meditation. Allow yourself at least half an hour simply to read it and read it repeatedly, identifying with different characters, including Jesus himself. Note down your feelings. Remember not to analyse those feelings. No judgement! Then, perhaps with the sentence, be there with Jesus, allowing the feeling, the atmosphere to surround you of his 'seeing', his 'understanding'. When you're finished, it's important to note down what happened in the period of meditation. Reflect not just on Christ's Passion, but your Passion.

- - -

130.

THE PILGRIMAGE

It's too hot for walking and Francis keeps sitting down on the side of the path and putting his head in his hands. He won't tell me what's wrong. Even my offering him some bread and cheese doesn't work. He's putting his hand up to push me away. But by mid-afternoon he becomes so tired that he leans on my arm still with his head bowed. "I read early today of Peter's denial", he whispers. "And so...?", I ask puzzled. "I realise", he adds with a cough, "that I've given attention to so many pilgrim's on this path, but I've not been open to Christ in you." "In me?" I chuckle. Francis weeps and adds, "Yes, I enjoy your laughter but maybe you're hiding. Will you let me see Christ in you?"

Read the section: Matthew 26.69-75

THE REFLECTION

At least Judas didn't lie! Maybe his intentions were distorted. 'Betrayal', is a word that has a permanent condemnation to it. Peter, however, 'the rock' was a liar, as I am, even if I hope my lying is not too often and not too obvious! But there's a wonderful impetuosity and naïvety to Peter, perhaps a strange but important 'gift' for me. God spare me from the blandishments of sophisticated Christianity. Simplicity and lack of guile, however, doesn't mean denying my intellectual life and the questioning that that brings. The third denial and the cock crowing led to that moment so powerfully caught in J S Bach's Passions: both the St Matthew and St John Passion. The narrator, a tenor, sings the words 'wept bitterly' with musical and liturgical pathos which is unparalleled in musical history. That lowest of low moments, is a point of unfathomable reassurance. There's no place, therefore, even in my own denial of Christ, that I can go that Christ in his love has not already been! Despair and hope: the paradoxical experience of Christ.

I will come to You in the place of your greatest distance from God.

THE EXERCISE

Entering into silent meditation no matter how you are feeling is, as this pilgrimage may have emphasised, part of the basic daily practice. Your mood may be be that of wanting to do everything but be with God. You may want to put your hand up and simply dismiss prayer and meditation as a waste of time. It may be, on the other hand, that you're longing to enter this bleak moment with Peter as it touches your own personal experience. Whatever the feeling (or lack of it!), be faithful to your time of prayer and let yourself go into your centre. Even if your practice is established, don't imagine that denial and distance from God is going to cease being an issue for you. This passage is your own dark moment 'around a fire' like Peter, trying to stay anonymous, perhaps to have your own loneliness and maybe even hopelessness exposed gently and lovingly as in the Gospel. If you feel like weeping, then weep.

- - -

CHAPTER TWENTY SEVEN – MATTHEW 27

131.

THE PILGRIMAGE

We've been walking through the desert where nothing seems to grow, except for the occasional desolate-looking scrub. The pathway is caked and like cracked clay. Beside the road, family groups of refugees huddle on their haunches staring hopelessly at us as we pass. They have been fleeing for weeks from conflict that had been raging around them. It's as if they're waiting for some inevitable fate. My bottle has only a dribble of water at the bottom. Wrapped in cloth is my stale bread and hard cheese. I urge Francis to keep going and not stop for any of them, who want to speak and hold on to him. We also need to find something to eat and drink. Beside a ruined sheep pen, I give Francis a little bread and the bottle. Later in the afternoon, he's desperate for water. I realise, later, that he'd taken his food and drink back to the refugees. Christ of the alienated and destitute, and I have still not learnt, or don't want to!

Read the section: Matthew 27.1-10

THE REFLECTION

One of the greatest challenges to any legal system, even in supposedly sophisticated societies, is to ensure that the outcome of litigation is not engineered in advance. History is full of legal cases where evidence has been distinctly loaded or 'spun' in order to produce a desired outcome. After all, it can be said that an agile adversarial lawyer has the task of attempting to steer the mind of the court in a particular direction and not necessarily in that which is just. Even on a personal level, in a tense relationship, I want to be right and you wrong. Worse, I'm in danger of assuming that you need to have the 'Jesus Christ' that I want you to have. And even worse still, I might find myself using the Bible as spiritual justification for my own prejudices and desire for influence over others. My desires and their outcomes take precedence! So the intolerable guilt that welled up in Judas, when he realised that the case against Jesus was manipulated, was too much. What an end! A potter's field: a graveyard for foreigners. Maybe that's where Christ is to be found: the locus of greatest rejection! Otherwise what's the point of the story being included in the Gospel?

I would have the trust and courage to find You in the places of alienation.

THE EXERCISE

Where is it that you've felt, and perhaps still feel, most alienated? Remember that this question is to be asked in the context of you praying! So, first, remember to establish stillness and focus. Sit in stillness, breathe easily and keep your hands resting on your lap. Be with Judas as he goes through his agony in this passage. If you have the nerve, allow yourself to be Judas in this story. Then, recall times when you've felt alienated, particularly by your own behaviour, attitudes, even words. What's essential, as always, is to conduct this exercise in the presence of Christ. This may be a disturbing exercise and remember to share your experiences of it with someone you trust if you can. What lies at the heart of the exercise is to recall what your feelings were about Jesus Christ as you prayed.

- - -

132.

THE PILGRIMAGE

Francis loves this weather, particularly here looking down the side of a hill onto the lush fields below. "It's as if you and I have a glimpse of eternity". That's my attempt to be poetic. "Maybe," grunts Francis. "What's wrong with you?" I ask, feeling put down a little.

"You've been missing eternity right in front of your nose!" Right now, I want this pilgrimage to end! Down in the village, we walk through a little alley-way, being drawn by the sight of a woman hitting her drunken son with a stick. "He deserves what he gets," I mutter self-righteously. Francis adds with a scalding tone, "Maybe you're enjoying watching him being thrashed." So, Francis holds me by the shoulders and turns me to face the couple. "Look into their faces. Now see if you're having a glimpse of eternity." The stillness of our presence caught the eye of the woman, who broke down in tears at the tragedy of their poverty.

Read the section: Matthew 27:11-26

THE REFLECTION

Jesus doesn't even attempt to defend himself. I can sense Pilate's and the religious leaders' frustration. The notorious prisoner, Barrabas, may have been a Robin Hood figure, a psychopathic killer, a terrorist, or some liberation fighter. The admiration for him in the crowd isn't that surprising. There's that strange almost furtive admiration I have, if I'm honest, for such characters who are either idolised or feared. The movie industry thrives on them, as does the news media. And while all that's happening, Pilate's wife, like a Lady Macbeth, is desperate to remove Jesus away from the trial and from execution. His presence cuts right into her soul; feeling exposed in front of him, just as Herod's wife felt exposed in the presence of John the Baptist. Ah! That anxiety in me, that someone is going to blow my cover!

That You may turn My heart to stillness, Light and Truth.

THE EXERCISE

Imagine yourself to be there in the crowd, another anonymous figure. You're watching, hardly able to admit that you're enjoying the thrill of someone else's suffering. You're almost whispering to yourself that you're glad it's not happening to you. Worse, there's nothing like watching a good public humiliation and even execution. You watch the politicians squirm and the religious leaders sweat at the seeming calm of Jesus. Gradually, you're startled at your own distorted desires and you long for that 'skill' in Jesus to remain still in the face of all those self-obsessed psyches. But try imagining yourself as Pilate's wife: the anxiety; the alarm at what you see as inevitable from this show-trial. What is it from which, by 'washing your hands' will set you free? Try writing down your responses to this exercise in the form of a prayer, accompanying your writing and praying with the sentence.

- - -

133.

THE PILGRIMAGE

Perhaps in this small lake, we might get a wash. "We're about to meet someone who needs our help and support", Francis barks rather crossly. "A young man you'll meet has been running from village to village hoping not to be caught. Forget your sweat and dirt and pay attention to what we must be and do!" Francis quickly ushers me into a little stone bothy. There sits the young man shivering from fear. He tells us that he has been wrongfully accused of raping a young woman in a nearby hamlet. I draw Francis aside. "But what can we do for him?" Through the door comes a man in his forties, who has been walking in silence not far from us for days. Francis recognises him. "Go with Francis", the older man whispers to the young man. In my alarm, I whisper to the older man, "But you. They will come for you instead". "Go!", the older man urges. Later, anxiously I complain, "Well, Francis, we did nothing there" Francis adds, "Really? Maybe you'll have to do the same one day for someone: take someone else's place." The Christ-like life indeed.

Read the section: Matthew 27:27-31

THE REFLECTION

Out of sight; out of mind. The Praetorium is a place of exclusive importance. Crowds would be assembling for a spectacle. Torture could be applied here without censure. The intention would've been to cause maximum fear and humiliation for Jesus. What we know of the Jewish experience of the Holocaust was that those who were led to the Gas Chambers, were first stripped and left trying to cover themselves, reducing humanity to futility, in fact eradicating humanity itself. Jesus remained in silence, fully exposed. A purple cloth was thrown over him, to hide his nakedness: the royal colour and, ironically, the colour of healing. The thorns of the crown thrust onto his head, wouldn't only cause bleeding but constant pain. Derision followed; designed to eradicate any sense of respect. So here we have a bewildering collection of images: royalty, healing, physical torture, humiliation, defencelessness. His own clothes were put back on him, perhaps because the crowd might grow angry with the soldiers for abusing the precious and expensive purple, the sign of royalty. With someone else's phlegm dripping down his cheeks, the rest was inevitable. And, there am I watching an equally culpable spectator.

I would acknowledge Your Love within me that I may see it in those around me.

THE EXERCISE

Perhaps this brutality comes to you too easily, as you're exposed daily to similar images of violence, directly or indirectly. What's much more challenging is to imagine Jesus' composure. The Passion narrative is pointing you to who Jesus is: the Love of God in the darkest and most distant place imaginable from that love – the ultimate in paradox. So, having read the passage carefully, slowly and entered its experience, move into silent prayer with the sentence and allow the Love of God in the distant place of human violence to be the focus of the silence. Remain there in the silence with Jesus, who remains with you, despite whatever agony you or those you're aware of, have experienced directly or indirectly.

- - -

134.

THE PILGRIMAGE

This pilgrimage for Francis isn't just about his own spiritual journey. "What do you think a spiritual journey is?" he'd asked earlier on the pilgrimage. He wasn't really expecting an answer. For him, it seems to me, this moment is where the attention and the intention must be. Here is God, although, he would add, "You won't see him, for if you did, it wouldn't be God." What then is there in this pilgrimage other than an eventful and memorable journey? And this morning I've the answer. Francis is leaning against an old tree, shielding himself from a hail-storm. He's holding a piece of torn paper folded up, as if it's his most treasured possession. "There's a name here. It's the name of a woman whose months-old baby died before we left on pilgrimage. I've been keeping it in my copy of the gospel." "But why do you need the paper?" "Because she wrote on it; she touched it. It's a direct connection to her. And so she's been with me all the way, as she asked." "Oh dear!" I exclaim. "I've just realised how many letters and notes like that I've just thrown away." Francis winks at me.

Read the section: Matthew 27.32-38

THE REFLECTION

There's no point in my pretending, I find the Christian Way bewildering. This section is particularly bewildering. Many seem to have followed Jesus, and still do, with little or no choice. Simon of Cyrene is one such. After the brutal abuse that he suffered, Jesus was obviously beyond carrying anything, let alone a heavy cross. Maybe it was the inevitability of his death that was also weighing too much. There's no telling what Simon of Cyrene felt or said. After all, for the Gospel narrative, obedience in following Jesus was of ultimate importance, pushing all other considerations into insignificance. And what obedience! Jesus has had his clothing removed. It may be that Jesus was completely naked on the Cross. For me, this is an image of God completely exposed and reduced to a squalid and humiliating wreck. I've tried saying "This is Jesus..." and know that it sticks in my throat. And to add to the excruciating experience, look at the company God keeps even at His death!

In My gift of stillness within You, I call You to open all of yourself to My Love.

THE EXERCISE

Maybe you can recall a time when you were asked to 'carry' someone's load, either literally or metaphorically. Maybe someone asked you to carry their luggage, their shopping, or help move their furniture. Maybe someone asked you to represent them to some institution, some official; maybe to carry someone's pain with them. Relive an event when you felt you couldn't really refuse. Your Simon of Cyrene moment. Whose weight do you feel called to carry? Have you resisted it? Now, imagine Jesus asking you to carry somebody, something, even his cross for him. Perhaps you're embarrassed at being associated with: 'Jesus, the King of the Jews'. Remember to review your time of prayer and imagining.

- - -

135.

THE PILGRIMAGE

A crowd of pilgrims appears to be making its way to some festival. Standing on a pavement is a young woman, cheeks soiled with tears, her baby wrapped in a filthy shawl and crying with hunger. The door of an adjacent house slams shut: "You're pilgrims, aren't you? Do something for this slut! Why don't you pray for her?" came a laughing comment from a window. "She's a whore and her child is a whore's child". Oh! That word whore flung at women down the ages. Two pilgrims as they pass her, haughtily turn their backs, adding with obsequiousness, "You ought to have been on the pilgrimage with us, repenting of your filth." Francis immediately rushes up to her, hugs her and kisses her on the forehead. I'm embarrassed. He takes the child from her and urges her to join him. "Come with me. You are a pilgrim with us. We will find warmth for the night". The other pilgrims? Some had gone, others looked on with withering laughter of self-righteousness. 'Probably her pimps", they sneer.

Read the section: Matthew 27.39-44

THE REFLECTION

To pass by is for me to be a spectator at a safe distance. From there I can join in the finger-pointing. Watching a drunken brawl on a city street can call forth from me dismissive accusations from that cold distance of being in the crowd. As I join in the hymn of condemnation, I realise the dark confusion and violence of my own soul. When the pain is happening to someone else, so often it comes with temporary relief for me. The jeering and laughing continues: 'Save yourself!' Here's an appeal that has echoed down history. A party atmosphere forms as jibe after jibe, including quotes from the Old Testament, gather pace and volume. 'He has put his trust in God'. Death by a thousand sneers, takes my gaze away from those who are crucified with Jesus in their dying.

Open the eyes of My Heart that I may see with clarity Your Love in the despised.

THE EXERCISE

Use the sentence to still yourself for a few moments. Go back to a time when you were jeered at; when you were powerless, belittled, humiliated. Relive the feelings. See the people; listen to what's being said to you or about you. Notice the looks on faces around you. Imagine Christ there with you. Do not do anything, just be with the experience, watch and feel in your prayer. Recall now the time when you've rejected and participated in jeering behaviour towards someone else. See Christ with that person. This exercise isn't about shame or guilt. It's simply about being aware of the power of being sucked into group destructive behaviour. Allow Christ to be the dominant 'centre' of your prayer as he becomes an instrument that 'short-circuits' the dark energies of back-biting and jeering. Remember to take note of your feelings and reactions. Above all, do not accuse yourself, just notice. This is your Passion!

- - -

136.

THE PILGRIMAGE

The snow covered landscape is now piercingly painful to look at in the bright sun. Francis' fingers are blue with cold. His breath is laboured. This morning, he'd been invited to speak about our pilgrimage in a village church, we were passing. Instead, he quietly chided the congregation that they were sitting there well-clothed and protected. "Homeless families are struggling to find warmth and you expelled them from the Church after they had been sleeping at the back overnight." The priest was furious. "You've taken gross advantage of my invitation to you to speak!" Francis replied for all to hear: "You're right! And I haven't started yet!" So, we huddled with the families, until we were thrown out of the town for breach of the peace. "Where's God now?" I asked almost resentfully. Francis replied, "That's not even a question."

Read the section: Matthew 27:45-56

THE REFLECTION

The cry of God. Here is Jesus, God in History crying across the whole Universe, audible in every corner of it, even paradoxically in the silence. Forsaken, Christ accompanies all those who feel abandoned by God; all those who experience His absence, including me. In the blackest of black holes somewhere in space, the cry still echoes: "My God, why have you forsaken me?" Yes, it's a quotation from a psalm and the cry can be explained away, but to no one's satisfaction. The question 'Why?' is by its very nature, never met with a satisfactory answer. God enters his own abandonment. He distances himself from himself. In the middle of the terrifying earthquake and storm, at the moment of abandonment, the centurion recognises and, further, acknowledges Jesus as the "Son of God". Bewildering indeed.

That in the places of fear, desolation and the experience of Your absence, I may remain there and wait on You.

THE EXERCISE

The Passion narrative brings you face to face with, perhaps, the starkest experience of all, to be awake at least to the possibility that you're experiencing or have experienced what it is to be an atheist. Atheism isn't simply a denial that that God exists, it's much more intense than that. It's the sense of the complete absence of God. Many of the great men and women of faith, however, seem to have experienced the absence of God. So allow yourself to experience in this moment of silent prayer a time when you not only did not believe in God, [or maybe – do not!], but felt [feel!] the weight of his absence. Then feel yourself 'cry out' with Jesus your sense of being abandoned. 'My God, why have you forsaken me?' Remain with that experience. You may find it's supportive to share your experience with someone else.

- - -

137.

THE PILGRIMAGE

A delicate looking man, wealthy-looking, dressed too smartly for the pilgrimage, joins us. Some distance back, he'd heard Francis give a talk in a barn about the essentials in being Christian: to pray and to love. He wants to know more. Our new companion, takes us into an inn and buys us a hearty supper. "Well. Not surprising, given the expensive look of him", I whisper to Francis. "Generosity is generosity, no matter who gives it," Francis growled. An old man approaches our host and insults him for his wealth and the lack of wear and tear on his face and hands. Francis turns to the old man and growls again, this time out loud. "Your skin is hard and cracked from hard work and hard weather, but so is your heart and your mind. This man has opened his heart to the risk of the Love of God."

Read the section: Matthew 27.57-61

THE REFLECTION

A burial place, particularly for wealthy and powerful Jews, would not only be in keeping with their life-style but also be a place of permanence, where they could be remembered. In that sense, the memory of the dead person would live on in others. This is a common practice in many cultures. So it was a considerable sacrifice for Joseph of Arimathaea to make his own tomb available for Christ. Legend has it that Joseph came to Britain with the Holy Grail, that mythological sacred chalice in which the blood of Christ was collected. Some who are affected by Celtic Christianity feel Joseph and the sacredness of the Grail brought, directly, Jesus' life through Europe. No matter whether or not this can be factually demonstrated or not, there's a hunger for a taste, a glimpse of the Presence of Jesus' life 'here'. This intriguing 'walk on' part for Joseph of Arimathea in the Passion narrative is perhaps a deep reassurance to those who feel at some distance from the centre of the story.

I would hold all I am and have before You in obedience to Your Love.

THE EXERCISE

This intriguing narrative is one in which silence is so demonstrative of love, gentleness and generosity. The two Marys sitting opposite the tomb create that wistful image of looking and listening with complete attention. In this exercise, in your own imagination, go back to a time when you were silent and were able to look and listen. What did it feel like for you? What was happening? Where in your life now do you feel you are being called to be a listener: someone who looks and gives attention? Give a little time to an occasion when you didn't listen or look, when perhaps that might have been helpful. Now, in prayer, what do you have which is most precious to you, that you would give out of love, out of love for Christ?

- - -

138.

THE PILGRIMAGE

I wish Francis would avoid this troubled territory, but he reminds me that a pilgrim must be faithful to where the path leads, including into the depths of darkness. Early this morning, a crowd passes the home that had welcomed us earlier. We quickly move among them to discover why they're looking so disturbed. They're holding aloft a painting of a young person who had spoken out against oppressive local leadership and had, as a result, been murdered for his courage. "What was the young person's greatest quality?" Francis asks. I'm feeling particularly puzzled as to know what to say, but I try. "Gentle integrity and inner strength, perhaps?" "Yes, I suppose that'll do, but it doesn't tell half the story", responds Francis, "A painting carried aloft gets deeper." "But why?", I ask. "It's the face of Christ in the young man summoning you to live gentle integrity yourself. Who knows? Someone may carry your painting aloft, and see the face of Christ in you." Francis laughs. I don't!

Read the section: Matthew 27:62-66

THE REFLECTION

One of the ways of undermining the humanity of those who are a threat, even when they're dead, is not to name them, but to label them. A name brings intimacy, immediacy. A label distances. The Christian Churches find it all too easy to label rather than to name. Labelling someone is an attempt to ensure that we're protected from what seems alien. This is, of course, in total contrast to the Christian dynamic, which is to love the alien. So Jesus, in the tomb is labelled as an 'imposter', a sham. What is more, giving him the label of a 'leader of the people' suggests that he's more powerful when dead than when alive. So sealing Jesus' tomb was intended to erase Jesus memory, let alone undermine any story of resurrection.

I would know intimately the life of Christ within Me, in my memory, my Praying and my Living.

THE EXERCISE

One of the tragedies of modern genocidal conflict, isn't just the destruction of a people, but erasing as much as possible, the memory, the history of that people: shredding the papers, burning the libraries, sometimes literally, that told its story. The numbing fear of nuclear holocaust is not simply about millions, maybe billions of deaths and the turning of the earth to glass, but the erasure of any memory of humanity: the sealing of our tomb. That's why this passage is perhaps the most chilling of all in the New Testament. The sealing of the tomb, at least in intention, is the final destructive act as it suffocates hope. What history of your life do you regard as essential and would be lost behind 'the sealed tomb'? What would you do in order to keep the memory alive, so that what may seem lost at your death may be 'unsealed'? Use the sentence to enter the exercise prayerfully.

- - -

CHAPTER TWENTY EIGHT – MATTHEW 28

139.

THE PILGRIMAGE

"Nothing to eat for two days. What are we going to do, Francis?" He doesn't bother replying. After a few hours, we eventually arrive at a friendly inn. Sitting by a fire and after a huge plate of broth and some fresh bread, we both fall fast asleep, waking just before dawn. Francis looks pale. As we set out, I ask him about his first experience of Christ. "It was early one morning, just like this, when my mother woke me as she always did with the words: 'Christ has risen', to which the expected response was, 'He is risen indeed'. At Easter, we were allowed to anwer with a shout 'Alleluia!'. One morning, I asked my mother where I could find this Risen Christ. She replied: 'He's going ahead of you.' So my experience, my friend, is that Christ is always just ahead of me." "Just out of sight?" I add in an attempt to be smart. Francis remains silent for a while, but then smiles and says, "The soup and bread went before you and waited on you." Whose turn is to be short now?

Read the section: Matthew 28.1-8

THE REFLECTION

Jesus' raising isn't given detail in this section. All I'm left with is observing the empty tomb and trying to make sense of the bewildering news: 'He is not here.' I'm silenced, but not by either naked acceptance or rejection of the resurrection. My silence is a growing awareness that my acceptance of the resurrection, tentative though it may be, is based on the lives and witness of those who experienced the Risen Christ. I use the term raising for the resurrection in preference to risen, as it isn't a single instant event, although there were resurrection events experienced. There has always been a drive to make the resurrection of Christ a matter of certainty in order that the facts can be spelt out. When the Resurrection narratives are spelt out as facts, of course, there's bound to be dissatisfaction. This story creates breathless expectation and hope, not certainty, like a child constantly delighted with what may lie round the next corner. With certainty, it seems to me, there's no faith, let alone hope and love. 'Now He is going ahead of you'.

Be silent and ponder My Presence which enlivens, raises You; goes ahead of You to guide You.

THE EXERCISE

Here you are again, confronted with that constant theme of fear which seems to pervade this pilgrimage.

Although this exercise has been used earlier on the pilgrimage, recall a time when you've been deeply afraid. Who's involved in this memory? Where are you? What's the cause of the anxiety? Be as observant as you can. Blame no one in this exercise, least of all yourself. Now read this section from Matthew carefully and maybe several times. Stop whenever a phrase or a word captivates you. Notice the tomb. Allow your imagination to picture every detail, every feeling associated with that detail. Listen to the words of the angel to the women. Allow your imagination to be free. Where would you go now? What's your first reaction? Note down as much of your experience of this exercise as you can recall. He is going before you!

- - -

140.

THE PILGRIMAGE

"D'you know, I think it'll be important for you and I to arrive at the completion of our pilgrimage by night", Francis almost whispers as we climb up steep valleys, presumably the last of the pilgrimage. "Why, by night?" "Well, you and I will be parting. I want to greet the dawn with you, in that stillness which we've shared on the way; that moment in the early part of the day, when the heart is most ready to receive the mystery of

Christ." I reflect for a while. "I do remember. We started many days of the pilgrimage in the dark, so that as we got into our stride, the dawn welcomed us constantly." Francis adds, "It's as if the hope of the dawn, the resurrection, is written into the cycle of the universe itself."

Read the section: Matthew 28.9-10

THE REFLECTION

So, there's a simple list of demands in this section: 'Do not be afraid… Go… Tell…' Jesus doesn't say, 'Let's talk about your fear' or 'Now look, my friends, you oughtn't to be afraid.' He makes a straight demand, as if he expects it, without hesitation, to be followed. Jesus suddenly comes to meet the women. The brothers 'must leave for Galilee.' No 'please' or 'perhaps', but another demand. Now, Galilee is where those Jesus called were first formed as disciples. So going back to Galilee is about returning to their first significant encounter with Jesus. So, I wonder about my first 'Galilee moment'. If the disciples return to Galilee opened up for them God's immediate gift of love and grace, enabling them to perceive, to feel the mystery of the resurrection, then I assume that same return will bring something of the same for me.

I would return to the first hint of Your Presence within Me and wait on Your Rising within Me. *Goe*

THE EXERCISE

As has been the case throughout this pilgrimage, memory is of vital importance. If Galilee would stimulate the memory of the disciples as to their first experience of Jesus, where would your 'Galilee moment' be? Where would be the experience, the first hint of Christ, in the detail of your personal life? Don't overlook anything, no matter how trivial. There's no detail, no fragment of your life that is lost in the presence of Christ. Even a crumb of burnt toast in your memory might unloosen a whole array of delight or maybe apprehension about your experience. One useful and enjoyable way of enabling the exercise to be given the time that's needed for it, is to go for a walk by yourself. Take a little notepad or, perhaps, a camera or sketch book. Don't be afraid to talk to Christ. Watch, listen, observe, note, pray. Return to your 'Galilee moment'. And, of course, you'll discover more than one, but one's quite enough!

- - -

141.

THE PILGRIMAGE

"This is the last stage of the pilgrimage". Francis points towards the city that lies on the side of the hill a few miles ahead of us. "I don't want this pilgrimage to end." I whimper feeling nostalgia already. "Will we see each other again? I have this feeling, Francis, that you'll want to go your own way then." Francis has a sad look on his face too, but doesn't really answer, instead he asks, "What, my trusty friend, will you remember about pilgrimage?" I laugh slightly nervously. What would I not remember? So, with a faltering voice, fighting back tears, I try to answer. "Every single situation we've been in, from the ordinary to the extraordinary, from the difficult to the boring, from the exciting to the worrying, from the beautiful to the ugly, you've summoned me to reflect on the presence of God in it all." "Continue that and you'll never be separated from me. Like that other story of separation, however, don't hold on to me. Holding on, strangely, means you lose the essence of what you've been given. Remember what we've both learnt about possession and freedom."

Read the section: Matthew 28.11-15

THE REFLECTION

I've a temptation to let this section speak for itself. The last phrase refers to the Jews. Reference to the Jews in the Gospels has been approached by New Testament theologians in many ways. However, in the context of increased racial sensitivity and awareness of anti-Semitism, this passage leaves the sensitive reader feeling uncomfortable. The History of Christendom is one where complicity in anti-Semitism can never be explained away. There's an inclination of those in power, not to have injustices exposed. Church history is charged with such stories of duplicity, intrigue, fear and evasion. The passion narrative itself has been used as a means of projecting blame for the killing of Jesus on the Jews. For me, the story of the empty tomb leaves a question mark on me as to my participation in racism. And that awareness is an urgent task. The resurrection, indeed, is a constant challenge to all posturing of power. The empty tomb is not a vacant tomb. It's filled with expectation, waiting.

That Your raising may instil Courage in Me to be set Free and be made Whole.

THE EXERCISE

You may have found it difficult in some of the exercises on this pilgrimage, to admit that you've been involved in the undermining of someone; a relationship, as has been suggested, that has made you feel jealousy. For most of us, however, there's that blushing remembering of our collusion in someone else's hurt or belittlement. Even if you've been spared such an experience, you can certainly imagine it. Imagine a scene of hiding and fear in which you've wanted to deny someone else's humanity in any way. Now imagine yourself wanting to find a way of denying Christ's rising. But remember Christ is used to being denied, being undermined.

- - -

142.

THE PILGRIMAGE

"So here we are. The pilgrimage is concluded". But Francis holds up a finger to warn me. "Remember one of the many lessons of the gospel we've had in our pockets, about possession. To say you've concluded the pilgrimage is to turn it into a personal possession. 'My pilgrimage'. And that closes off the dream." After a pause, Francis says mystifyingly, "Place the palms of your hands against this wall and gently lean." "Why?" I ask bewildered. "Stay there for a while. When you take your hands away, open your hands and spread your arms with the gift of God's incomprehensible love which radiates even from the stone of this wall!" These are the last words I hear from Francis.

Conclusion

That's not quite true. Throughout the pilgrimage I've shared with Francis and many others, I've tried to keep notes of his comments and some of his activities, which I hope I've shared with you, who are making a pilgrimage on The Way of Christ in your own way. The sound of these comments perhaps echo around the 'hillsides' and accompany you on your path of Christ-like living, or I hope they do. So I place my hands again on the wall and feel the cold sandy texture almost caressing my palms. And where have we come to as we 'touch the shrine' of our pilgrimage? Back where we began, but strangely, just a little higher, maybe only a centimetre or two, as if we're caught up on a barely discernible spiral. I turn after a while with my hands outstretched. I'm alone. Or am I?

Read this final section.: Matthew 28.16-20

THE REFLECTION

'Setting out for Galilee'. This is a vitally important indicator. For the disciples make their way to the point where and at which they first encountered Jesus, or more accurately, were encountered by Jesus. So the memory of the story of their discipleship is key. The experience of the raising of Christ that they had at the place of encounter, was an opening, or using a more traditional word, revelation. So the significance of the raising enfolds them in the place of recollection. The raising, as I've tried to show, can't be laid out for examination or charted historically. The raising of Christ is, nevertheless, experienced in time. The experience of following, of friendship, of betrayal, of rejection, of anxiety, of agony and painful death and the raising were the environment in which they had made the pilgrimage which eventually brought them to be messengers of the gospel and witnesses of its truth, that lies in the Word beyond words. They became apostles. On going to Galilee, they couldn't return to the exact spot, for that's the journey of nostalgia and perhaps even self-indulgence. As apostles they would have authority, the authenticity of the Presence of Christ, awakening them to realise that they've returned to their initiation but they're lifted, being raised themselves, caught up in the slip stream of the raising.

My Love of You gathers You to the place of encounter that You may move out in that Love to others.

THE EXERCISE

Find a stone that you can hold that's not too heavy, but substantial enough that you can feel its weight and size. The age of the rock perhaps from which it came may well be immeasurable. You had to lift it from somewhere in order to hold it. This was a raising. It's also a return for you to Galilee. Here's an experience of your beginning! The very stuff of the earth from which you came and to which you're now returning. You haven't entirely returned, but have moved upwards, been lifted, raised slightly, as if you're on a spiral. Perhaps only centimetres. So, as you hold the rock, remember again your first experience of God, no matter how trivial and particular it was. Relive it. Tell the story of the encounter. Now replace the rock and lay you hands open as your commitment to allow the gift of your encounter to be passed on. Someone else may pick it up and have their return story to tell. 'I am with you to the end of time'. This pilgrimage isn't for you alone. It's for 'the other', whoever that other is that God has given you. After all, in your loving, you're immediately with God, probably you'll never be closer, for God is love. Keep your eyes open. The pilgrimage, of course, hasn't come to an end. Here, at the end, you've moved along, around but a little higher, to make friends again with your origins, known and unknown.

A blessing from the Island of Iona, attributed to St Columba:

> *'Be the great God between your two shoulders*
> *To protect you in your going out and your coming in.*
> *Be the Son of Mary ever near your heart,*
> *And be the perfect Spirit upon you pouring.*
> *Oh, the perfect Spirit upon you pouring.'*

Lightning Source UK Ltd.
Milton Keynes UK
UKOW01f1128270717
306167UK00001B/54/P

9 781911 035473